DEAfNESS AND MENTAL HEALTH

of related interest

Counselling – The Deaf Challenge
Mairian Corker
ISBN 1 85302 223 3

'The cunning finger, finely twined. The subtle thread that knitteth mind to mind. And by an arch no bigger than the hand, Truth travels over to the silent land.'

Anonymous

DAVID SCOTT, a blind boy, and SARAH ARMSTRONG, a dumb girl,
PUPILS IN THE ULSTER INSTITUTION,
Conversing together.
Drawn from life and presented to the Society for the benefit of its funds by

MAY, 1838.

Augⁿ Edouart

DEAFNESS AND MENTAL HEALTH

John Denmark

Foreword by Roy McClelland

Jessica Kingsley Publishers
London and Bristol, Pennsylvania

The right of John Denmark to be identified as author of this work has been asserted by him in accordance with the Copyright, Designs and Patents Act 1988.

First published in the United Kingdom in 1994 by
Jessica Kingsley Publishers Ltd
116 Pentonville Road
London N1 9JB, England
and
1900 Frost Road, Suite 101
Bristol, PA 19007, U S A

Copyright © 1994 John Denmark
Foreword copyright © 1994 Roy McClelland

Library of Congress Cataloging in Publication Data
A CIP catalogue record for this book is available from the Library of Congress

British Library Cataloguing in Publication Data
Denmark, John C.
Deafness and Mental Health
I. Title
362.4

ISBN 1-85302-212-8

Printed and Bound in Great Britain by
Biddles Ltd., Guildford and King's Lynn

CONTENTS

Acknowledgements

The author wishes to thank:

The Royal National Institute for Deaf People for
permission to reproduce figures 1, 2, 3 and 4.

The Trustees of the Ulster Society for Promoting the
Education of the Deaf and Dumb, and the Blind for
permission to use the illustration which appears as the
frontispiece to the book, and on the cover.

FOREWORD

To suffer the dual problems of deafness and mental illness seems extremely bad luck. However, for those who work closely with deaf people, their increased vulnerability to psychological problems and difficulties is already acknowledged. This is particularly so for those whose deafness dates from early life. Severe deafness affects not only speech and communication but can also have major consequences for educational, emotional and social development. It is surprising, therefore, that in most so-called developed countries, the mental health needs of severely deaf people is very much a case of 'out of sight, out of mind'. The deficiencies of service development are paralleled in the inadequacies of training and education for health care professionals. A major gap is the lack of clear guidance on the mental health issues of deaf people.

John Denmark addresses this void with a clarity, comprehensiveness and authority that only a life-time's professional work dedicated to the needs of the deaf people can bring. Those of us who have had the privilege of listening to his lectures have held onto every word. At last we have John Denmark's written work which will secure for the next generation a major source of wisdom, common sense and sound advice. This book is a must for all health care professionals, particularly those whose practice brings them into contact with deaf people.

Roy McClelland
Professor of Mental Health
Queen's University of Belfast

INTRODUCTION

'All tragedy is a failure of communication.' (Wilson 1956)

Since ancient times, attitudes to deaf people have been veiled in ignorance and superstition. For example, Aristotle believed that children who were born deaf were 'incapable of reason' and in medieval Britain deaf people without speech were classed as idiots, and were prevented from managing their own affairs or bequeathing their property. Even today, most people are unaware of the psychosocial implications of the different types of deafness and do not consider it to be a serious disability. Yet Helen Keller (1933), who became both deaf and blind in the second year of her life, believed deafness to be 'by far the greater misfortune'. Similarly, Samuel Johnson (1775), described deafness as 'one of the most desperate of all human calamities'. Best (1943) pointed out that humour frequently reflects public attitudes and observed that, while the blind are only to be seen in tragedies, the deaf are often seen in comedies.

There are a number of reasons why the psychological and sociological implications of deafness are not generally understood. Deafness is not visible. A deaf person will appear to the casual observer to be no different from anyone else, while the inappropriate answer of a partially deaf person who has misunderstood may appear to be humorous, or may cause irritation. Deafness is a blanket term which covers a wide variety of different conditions with markedly different implications depending upon many factors. These include degree of deafness, age and rate of onset and the intelligence, personality and life situation of the person affected. For example, profound deafness from birth or early age can, without proper intervention, affect the child's whole development, while the sudden onset of deafness in adult life can be an extremely traumatic experience requiring many readjustments. The former constitutes a sensory deficit, the latter a sensory deprivation. They have entirely different implications and cannot be equated. Yet another important factor has been the denigration of the use of sign language by teachers of deaf children.

Unfortunately, few members of the caring professions receive any training in the psychological and sociological implications of deafness. Medical students, for example, study the anatomy and physiology of hearing and audiometry, audiology and otology, but few receive any training in communication disorders or in the psychological and sociological aspects of different types of deafness. Moreover, most text books of psychiatry make no reference to the difficulties which may be encountered in the diagnosis and treatment of some deaf people with mental health problems.

Deaf people are probably no more prone to mental disorders than hearing people. However, very few workers in the field of mental health are conversant with the psychological and sociological aspects of deafness, and the consequences can be tragic. Conversely, few workers in the field of deafness have any formal training in mental health issues, so that mental disorders are often not recognised and remain untreated.

This book is not an academic one but has been written primarily for workers who may meet a deaf person in the course of their work – general practitioners, psychiatrists, paediatricians, psychologists, nurses and social workers. However, it will also be of help to those who work in the field of deafness – otologists, audiologists, teachers of deaf children, hearing therapists and social workers with deaf people as well as those who work in the special field of mental health and deafness. It does not deal with the physical aspects of hearing or deafness, apart from listing the causes of deafness and the commoner syndromes associated with it. The latter are important because deafness may be associated with disabling conditions.

The chapter on Psychiatry and Deaf People presupposes some understanding of mental health issues. Accordingly, a glossary is appended at the end of the book to assist those readers who do not have this knowledge.

Although deafness is a blanket term covering many different degrees and types of deafness occurring in many different settings, it is possible to generalise to some extent, and an attempt has been made to describe the different implications of deafness which dates from early life and that which is acquired after speech and language have developed. The book also deals with the important issue of deaf people with disabilities, especially those who are mentally or visually impaired. Deafness is often confused with other conditions which affect the development of speech and language and these are described.

Mental disorders include reactions to stress, mental illness, mental impairment and disorders of personality. They can occur in a setting of any type of deafness. When there are communication difficulties, diagnosis and treatment can be extremely difficult and special psychiatric services are necessary if deaf people are to be correctly diagnosed and treated. Unfortunately, few countries have such services, and where they do exist they are not fully comprehensive. The book describes both the clinical and service aspects of mental disorders when they affect people who are deaf and highlights the great need for the development of special mental health services for deaf people in all countries.

The field of crime and deafness presents complex problems and some aspects are covered.

Social workers with deaf people have very important roles to play and the need for them to receive training, not only in social work and deafness but also in mental health issues, is underlined.

Much confusion has arisen in the past because workers in the field of deafness have used terms with different meanings. To avoid such confusion, an appendix is included which deals with the meaning of terms and the classification of different types of deafness.

DISABILITY

When writing about deafness, a decision has to be made whether or not to consider it to be a disability. As has been pointed out elsewhere, deafness is a blanket term covering many different degrees and types of deafness with different implications. There can be no doubt that those who become deaf in adult life have a disability. However, many preverbally deaf people hold the view that they are not disabled but are a cultural and linguistic minority. When using the term 'deafness' in a generic manner, it is convenient to regard it as a disability.

CHAPTER ONE

PSYCHOLOGICAL, SOCIOLOGICAL AND CULTURAL ASPECTS OF DEAFNESS

'You never really understand a person until you consider things from his point of view... until you climb into his skin and walk around in it.' (Lee 1960)

INTRODUCTION

Deafness may be present at birth or be acquired at any age – in childhood, in adolescence, in adult life or in the senium. It can be of any degree, from a slight impairment in one ear to total bilateral deafness. It may be of acute, subacute or insidious onset. It may vary from time to time. It often gets worse. It can sometimes be cured. It can often be alleviated.

Deafness can affect the genius or the mentally impaired, the introvert or the extrovert, the single or the married person, the artisan or the scholar. The effects must necessarily vary. Of particular importance are the age of onset and the degree of deafness. Prelingual profound deafness is a sensory deficit while post lingual deafness is a sensory deprivation. They cannot be equated.

This chapter covers some of the problems of those whose deafness dates from birth or early age (preverbal deafness) and those who become deaf in adolescence or in adult life. It includes the important issue of methods of communication in the education of deaf children and makes some comment on deaf children who have disabilities. It does not include the difficulties of 'hard of hearing' people or those whose deafness develops progressively as these are well covered in other works.

PREVERBAL PROFOUND DEAFNESS

'The wonder of necessity which Nature worketh in men that
are borne deaf and dumbe; who can argue and dispute
rhetorically by signs, and with a kind of mute and logistique
eloquence overcome their... opponents; wherein some are so
really excellent, they seem to want nothing to have their
meanings perfectly understood.' (Bulwer 1644)

Profound deafness from birth or which occurs before the development of
speech and language presents an enormous barrier to the development of
speech and verbal language. To understand why this is so it is helpful to
consider the development of speech and language in hearing children.

Most hearing children are born into homes where people talk. The adults
talk to each other and they talk to the children. Hearing children are bathed
in verbal language. At first they babble but soon they learn to speak. To do
so they have to be able to hear speech and to monitor their own voices, both
in pitch and in volume. Soon they begin to internalise their speech, to
associate the words they say with people and with objects. By the end of
the first year most hearing children are able to say a few words but they are
able to understand much more, and by the age of four years they have a
vocabulary of some four thousand words and have mastered most of the
grammatical complexities of their native tongue.

Children who are profoundly deaf from early life cannot learn to speak
intelligibly. The main reason is that, being unable to hear, they cannot imitate
the speech of others or monitor their own voices. Another important factor
is that such children have a long preverbal stage. Some never achieve a
complete mastery of verbal language while others remain non-verbal.

At one time, the most important aspect of the development of communication for children with preverbal profound deafness was seen as the
difficulty they have in acquiring verbal language. They cannot develop verbal
language through hearing and must use another sensory modality. It is
believed by some workers that these children can acquire verbal language
through lipreading. However, lipreading is not easy because some of the
speech sounds are not accompanied by movements of the mouth and lips,
while for others the movements are the same for different sounds. More
important, lipreading presupposes a knowledge of verbal language which
children with early onset deafness do not possess. To illustrate this, consider
the situation if an excellent lipreader of English were to sit in front of a
television set in a foreign land with the sound turned off. He would find it
impossible to lipread a newscaster if he did not understand the language of

BROTHER

BIG

BRING or FETCH

BAD

BREAK

CRUSH

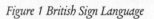

Figure 1 British Sign Language

that country. Preverbally profoundly deaf children cannot, therefore, acquire verbal language through lipreading.

It is also impossible for very young deaf children to acquire verbal language through the written word because literacy in English requires a degree of intellectual and neurological maturation. Children who are profoundly deaf from an early age are, therefore, unable to acquire functional verbal language in the vital formative years. They have a long preverbal stage and their first language should be their natural language – sign language. One deaf man whose hearing parents had no facility in sign language likened his early childhood to living in a goldfish bowl and watching them trying to communicate with him by opening and shutting their mouths!

Many preverbally profoundly deaf people do not acquire fluency in written English, which is their second language. However, they are able to communicate easily with other deaf people by sign language. Understandably, they reject the view that they are handicapped. Their perspective is that they are a linguistic and cultural minority.

Sign languages had their origins in gesture. They involve facial expression and movements of the fingers, hands, arms and body. Like verbal languages, different countries have their own sign languages.

Fingerspelling is a method of communicating verbal language by making different configurations and or movements of the fingers of one or both hands to depict the different letters of the alphabet. In the United Kingdom, in Australia and in New Zealand the two-handed alphabet is used (see Figure 2) while in the United States of America and most other countries a one-handed alphabet is employed (see Figure 3).

Learning to fingerspell is quite easy but learning to 'read' fingerspelling is a very different matter. It is different from reading the printed word where all the letters of the words are seen simultaneously. When reading fingerspelling only one letter is seen at a time, and then only fleetingly. Moreover, there is usually no perceived spacing between the words. Deaf people usually use fingerspelling for names and some nouns.

Most deaf people use a combination of sign language and fingerspelling, depending on who they are communicating with and their level of literacy in English. Sign language is used in most social situations, while in formal situations such as lectures and meetings a combination of the two methods is usually employed, especially if technical terms are used. Deaf people often refer to other deaf people and some hearing people by their sign names.

The difficulty for preverbally profoundly deaf children of acquiring literacy in English is illustrated in the following anecdote.

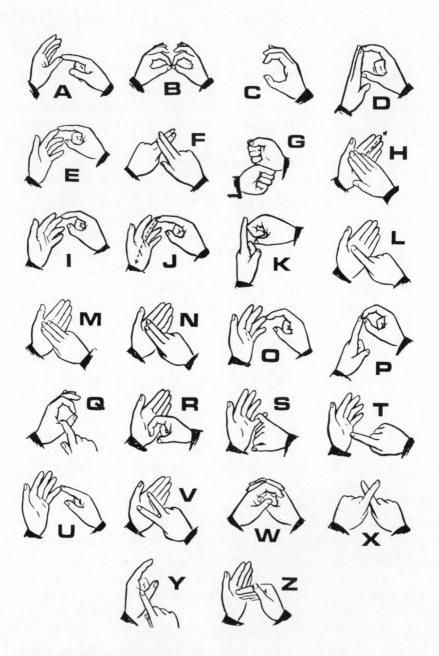

Figure 2 The British manual alphabet

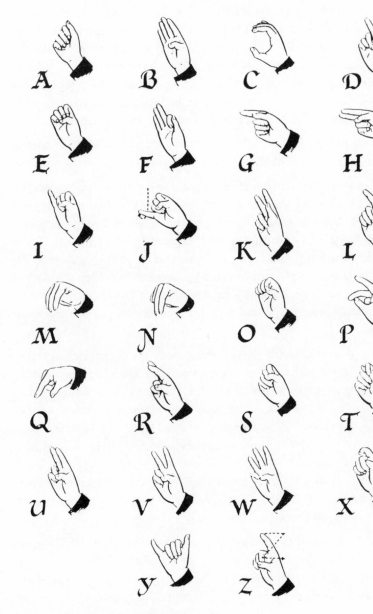

Figure 3 The one-handed manual alphabet

WI, an intelligent young man who had been profoundly deaf from birth, was admitted to Whittingham Hospital (in Preston, Lancashire) under the care of the author before the Department of Psychiatry for the Deaf was opened in 1968. He had been taught at a school for deaf children which adopted an oral approach to communication and his English language was poor. However, he was fluent in sign language and, within the limits of his verbal language, by fingerspelling.

W soon became friendly with a young female patient who had normal hearing and visited her home after she was discharged from hospital.

One morning the author was holding a meeting of staff in preparation for the opening of the Department. W used to join these meetings and enjoyed demonstrating his ability to communicate by sign language and fingerspelling. One day he told the meeting of a visit to the home of his new friend and that her father had given him a present. He produced a diary. The author asked him to name the object whereupon he made the sign for a book – holding the palms of his hands together and then opening them as though they were hinged at their lower edges.

W was then asked to fingerspell the name of the object. He fingerspelt 'b o o k'. The author asked its purpose. He replied, again using sign language, that he was not stupid. He knew it was not for reading but was for 'dates'. (The word 'date' was not in his vocabulary but he understood the concept and made the sign.) He was told that the object was a 'd i a r y', the words being fingerspelt. He was asked to remember the word. W commented that it would be easy to do so, making the sign for 'easy' by pressing the tip of his right index finger into his cheek. The following meeting W was keen to show that he remembered the word but fingerspelled 'd a i r y'.

As W had no auditory memory which would have enabled him to recall the sound of the word 'diary', his faulty recall of the order of the letters was understandable. (His poor English language was almost certainly the result of inappropriate methods of communication used at school.)

DEAF PEOPLE WITH DISABILITIES

Both congenital and acquired deafness commonly occur alone but they may be associated with disabilities. These may be due to hereditary or non-hereditary causes. Koenigsmark and Gorlin (1976) described many syndromes in which deafness is associated with one or more disabilities, while many of the factors responsible for non-hereditary deafness such as prematurity, birth injury and meningitis may cause more widespread brain damage.

The high incidence of deaf children with disabilities was highlighted in a study of 3000 pupils in schools for deaf children in countries of the European Community (Martin *et al.* 1978). This revealed that 29% had disabilities and that 9.9% were mentally impaired. The other common disabilities are motor disorders and visual impairments. Motor disorders may adversely affect the deaf child's ability to acquire communication skills. They may affect speech (anarthria or dysarthria) and/or fingerspelling and sign language (apraxia or dyspraxia). Some of the difficulties of those who are both visually and hearing impaired are dealt with in Chapter Two.

Mental impairments occurring in deaf people may be of any degree but there is one aspect that is of particular importance. Many hearing people have relatively minor degrees of mental impairment which are of a degree to preclude literacy in English. Nevertheless, they are able to acquire verbal language (i.e., English) through hearing. However, should persons with *preverbal* profound deafness have a mental impairment of a similar degree they will have no potential for verbal language. They will be unable to acquire verbal language through hearing or through the written word. They will remain non-verbal – they will have no potential for English language. The implications of this are important to understand because there will be a marked discrepancy between the innate intellectual potential of such children and their potential for literacy in English.

Many deaf children with minor degrees of mental impairment become emotionally and behaviourally disturbed if they are denied the opportunity to learn to communicate using sign language. So to do is deny them their natural and only opportunity to acquire an effective medium of communication (Denmark 1979, unpublished research).

> PL was referred at the age of 14 years 6 months for advice as to management. He had been born six weeks prematurely and had a birth weight of only 4 pounds 14 ounces. There was some neonatal distress. At six weeks he suffered from meningitis. He did not learn to speak and at the age of three years deafness was suspected. However, this was not confirmed until he was six years old when profound sensori-neural

deafness was diagnosed. He was tried with a binaural aid and had auditory training but without benefit. His behaviour became progressively more disturbed. Eventually his parents were unable to cope and he was admitted to a hospital for the mentally impaired. It was reported that he failed to settle and psychotropic medication brought about no change in his behaviour. The results of psychometric testing were thought to be unreliable because of his poor concentration and distractibility.

Some 12 months prior to referral P was involved in a programme using Makaton and it soon became obvious that he could be taught to communicate using this method. His behaviour immediately improved and he soon began to 'mimic' other patients and to help other more mentally impaired patients with their personal care.

P was profoundly deaf. He was only able to communicate at a very basic level by sign language. It appeared that most of his problems derived from lack of proper assessment and the provision of appropriate help. Unfortunately, his parents could not be traced.

It was recommended that P should be tried at a residential school for deaf children. Some 12 months later it was reported that there were no behaviour problems and that he was making good progress.

KG was referred at the age of 13 years. He had failed to speak and had been seen by a number of different specialists. As a young child he was described as 'hyperactive'. One audiologist thought he was not deaf and believed his intelligence quotient to be 'below 44'.

As a young child, K had spent two periods on trial at a school for mentally retarded deaf children, but was not accepted because of his disturbed behaviour, and at the age of eight years he was admitted to a hospital for the mentally impaired.

For some time after admission K continued to be disturbed. However, there were a number of members of staff who had acquired some facility in Makaton and he became involved in a group with other 'non-communicating' children. K's behaviour gradually improved to the extent that he was able to cooperate with audiometric testing which revealed severe bilateral sensori-neural deafness. It was also possible to demonstrate that he had some useful hearing with an aid, which he eventually accepted.

When examined by the author, K had acquired a small vocabulary of words through hearing and was able to respond to simple commands. He had also acquired some facility in sign language. However, in spite of intensive help he had remained illiterate in English.

K was considered to be both deaf and mentally impaired. However, there was no doubt also that exposure to sign language had brought about a considerable change in his behaviour. Moreover, although he was mentally impaired this was not of such a degree as had been thought, for on further psychometric testing he achieved a performance intelligence quotient of 68.

K was eventually transferred to a hospital for the mentally impaired with a deaf unit where he continued to make progress. He was eventually discharged to a hostel and was found a place in a sheltered workshop.

There is a high incidence of deafness among the mentally impaired. The exact incidence is difficult to determine. However, in a study in 19 of 143 hospitals for people with mental impairment with a total patient population of 37,137 patients the following distribution was found (Denmark 1979, unpublished research).

TABLE 1

Distribution of deaf patients in 143 hospitals
for the mentally impaired

Deaf without speech	737	2.0%
Deaf with speech	593	1.5%
Hard of hearing	1564	4.2%
Total	**2894**	**7.8%**

Of the 2894 patients who were either deaf or hearing impaired, 1031 (35%) used either sign language or gesture for communication purposes. In another study (Kropka and Williams 1966), it was found that 10.8% were either deaf or hearing impaired.

It is important that deaf children who are thought to be mentally impaired are properly assessed and that their parents are offered counselling and the opportunity to acquire sign language skills. It is also important to understand that, just as many hearing people with lesser degrees of mental impairment become mature and stable members of society, hold down routine jobs, marry and raise families, so too do many preverbally profoundly deaf people with mental impairments become stable and productive citizens. They have immense difficulty in communicating with hearing people but they are able to integrate with deaf people who use sign language.

THE EDUCATION OF DEAF CHILDREN

> 'Children wish for so much but can arrange so little of their
> own lives which are so often dominated by adults without
> sympathy for the children's priorities.' (Bettelheim 1990)

The earliest attempts to teach deaf children date back only to the sixteenth century when, in Spain, a Benedictine monk, Pedro Ponce de Léon (1520–1584) taught a few carefully selected pupils. There are references to sporadic attempts to teach deaf children in a number of countries from that time onwards but it was not until two centuries later that their education started to become systematised.

In the 1760s a French abbot named de l'Épee began to teach deaf children. He had become aware that deaf people without speech communicated effectively with each other by sign language and decided to use this method. At about the same time as de l'Épee was teaching deaf children by sign language in France, Samuel Heineke (1729–1790) was teaching in Germany using a purely oral/auditory approach. He decried the use of sign language, arguing that if deaf children were to take their place in society they had to speak and to lipread. Thus began the controversy between the 'oralists' on the one hand and those who believed in the use of sign language on the other.

The nineteenth century saw the development of schools for deaf children throughout Britain and America and the communication methods employed have varied in these schools, and in those of other counties also, since. In Germany, pure oral methods have been used since the time of Heineke. In Britain, some schools used oral methods while others used sign language until, towards the end of the last century, most schools adopted a purely oral/auditory approach.

Great impetus to the use of pure oral methods was imparted at an International Conference of Teachers of the Deaf which took place in Milan in 1890. One resolution which was passed with loud acclaim and for which the conference became a landmark was the following:

'The congress, considering the incontestable superiority of speech over signing in restoring the deaf mute to society, and giving him a more perfect knowledge of language, declares that the oral method ought to be preferred to that of signs for the education and instruction of the deaf and dumb.'

The French accepted this edict and became totally converted to the oral system after 1890.

Delegates from Britain were equally enthusiastic and, as a result, a new society, the Ealing Society, was established in the same year. Deaf children were then taught by the 'German method', as oralism was then described. Another society, the Association for the Oral Instruction of the Deaf and Dumb in Training Colleges of Teachers of the Deaf, had predated the Milan conference by ten years. In 1915 these two societies amalgamated. Later this body became known as the Oral Foundation but it too was absorbed, following the establishment of the National College of Teachers of the Deaf.

Teachers of deaf children in this country were first trained at Fitzroy Square, London. However, this closed when the Department of Audiology and Education of the Deaf opened at Manchester University. This department and the National College of Teachers of the Deaf adopted a purely oral/auditory approach to education until fairly recently. So emotive is the controversy over methodology that deaf children in some schools are still punished if they are found using fingerspelling or sign language.

The advent of the hearing aid gave further support to the case for oralism. It is, of course, true that hearing aids have been of enormous benefit to many deaf people of all ages. It is also true that hearing aids have enabled some deaf children who are severely deaf without aids to hear reasonably well with them. Unfortunately, the advent of hearing aids helped to perpetuate the myths that all deaf children have useful hearing for speech, can be educated by purely oral/auditory methods and can integrate into hearing society by becoming like hearing people. This is not so.

An example of the narrow oralist approach was that of the late Sir Alexander Ewing, one-time Professor of Audiology and Education of the Deaf, Manchester University and his wife the late Lady Ewing who, in a booklet published by the National Deaf Children's Society (1961) wrote: 'In recent years it has been shown very clearly that, through early and skilful training, in their homes and at school, many profoundly deaf children can learn to talk freely, in sentences, in clear speech, with natural voices'. Later, in the preface to a book entitled *Teaching Deaf Children to Talk* (Ewing and Ewing 1964), the same authors wrote 'Above all else this book expresses the conviction, reinforced by lifelong experience as teachers, that the highest priority for deaf children is learning to talk'. Even later, in giving evidence to the Lewis Committee on the Education of Deaf Children (1968), Sir Alexander stated, 'Only in exceptional circumstances would it be appropriate to consider introducing non-oral methods'. He said that he would 'regard combined methods as a last resort for children failing to achieve any score in language after all that was possible had been done for them'. In answer to questioning he said that an appropriate age to introduce such methods would be twelve years. He did not, evidently, appreciate the need for effective communication in the early formative years.

The oral approach to the education of deaf children held sway in almost all schools for deaf children in Britain until the 1970s when, following the concern of psychiatrists and psychologists working with deaf people, attitudes of teachers began to change. Of major importance was a seminar undertaken by the Royal National Institute for the Deaf in 1975 (Royal National Institute for the Deaf 1976).

Many schools now use sign language, but in different ways. Some adopt a 'bilingual' approach, using British Sign Language to teach, while others use signs to help 'support' teaching using English (Signs Supporting English). However, even today, the controversy continues. For example, the Department of Audiology and Education of the Deaf at Manchester University still adopts an oral/auditory stance, believing that sign language should not be used except with deaf children with disabilities, while the National Aural Group (1993) makes no mention of sign language in their advertisement. This states:

> 'It's a myth that deaf children must lead totally isolated lives in a world of silence. Disco music or Bach, opera or pop, Shakespeare or rep – all can be heard and enjoyed by deaf children… if we give them a chance. With expert help and the right hearing aids deaf children can grow up in a world of sound. They can learn to listen and speak for themselves. Deaf children can learn to talk in the same way that all children do – by learning to listen and by having adults talk and play with them.'

The controversy over methodology arose because some deaf children can be educated by oral/auditory methods, can learn to speak and lipread and can cope in hearing society. However, these are children who are partially deaf who have good hearing for speech with amplification or children who have become deaf postlingually.

The oralists decry the use of sign language and fingerspelling. They believe that it should be the aim of education to integrate all deaf children into hearing society. They believe, moreover, that if exposed to sign language and fingerspelling they will not be motivated to speak and to lipread. They do not understand the folly of this and do much damage by giving parents false and over-optimistic expectations.

To understand the problems of teaching deaf children certain issues need to be clarified. It is important, first of all, to discount the myth that all deaf children have useful hearing for speech with amplification. This is not the case. The benefits that have accrued from advances in audiology and the use of hearing aids are immeasurable. However, some children are totally deaf while others have residual hearing which, even when amplified, is of little or no help for speech discrimination (Denmark, F.G.W., 1973, personal communication). It is also necessary to understand the difficulties for preverbally deaf children in developing speech and verbal language and to compare the roles of teachers of deaf children with those of teachers of normally hearing children.

It is trite to say that education begins at home but it truly is the case. By the time hearing children start school they already have a good command of language and are able to communicate easily with others. Moreover, they have a store of general knowledge and have begun to acquire both social skills and moral concepts. The task of teachers of normally hearing children is, therefore, to teach their pupils to read and to write – to put into another form the verbal language they have acquired through hearing, to build upon knowledge already acquired, and to prepare them for life after they leave school.

The task of the teacher of deaf children is entirely different from the teacher of hearing children and can be formidable. If the children are preverbally severely or profoundly deaf and have been born into families with no other deaf members they may have little or no verbal language and their ability to communicate in any medium may be extremely limited. Indeed, their teachers' first task may be to give such children a medium through which they can communicate. Then, and only then, will they be able to teach them.

Preverbally profoundly deaf children have a long preverbal stage and the difficulties in teaching them using an oral approach has been reflected in their limited achievements. One study highlighted the problems of very young deaf children. Among 122 deaf and partially hearing children under the age of five years whose parents had not received any instruction in sign language, it was found that 57% relied exclusively on gesture, showing and pointing when communicating with their mothers (Gregory 1976). In another study of 360 children aged between 15 years and 16 years 6 months in schools for deaf and partially hearing children in England and Wales Conrad (1976) found that of those with hearing losses greater than 85 decibels, half had reading ages of less than 7 years 6 months, half lipread worse than the average hearing child and only 10% had intelligible speech. (It is likely that the latter 10% had useful hearing for speech with amplification.)

The essential problem is that while it may be relatively easy to decide whether or not sign language is to be the first language for some deaf children, for other children the issue may not be so clear. Some deaf children can hear well with hearing aids while others have great difficulty (severe deafness) or have no hearing at all even with amplification. The first language of the former will be English, of the latter it will be sign language. However, the decision as to method(s) for children who have moderate degrees of deafness is more difficult to make. It is, of course, important that full use is made of any residual hearing and that speech training is not neglected, but most of these children need sign language as well as English.

The teaching of speech is also a complex problem. Few, if any, preverbally profoundly deaf children will ever learn to speak intelligibly and many severely deaf children have poor oral skills. Valuable time can, therefore, be wasted in attempting to teach speech to some deaf children. Gesell (1956) wrote, 'Our aim should not be to convert the deaf child into a somewhat fictitious version of a normal hearing child, but into a well adjusted non-hearing child who is completely managing the limitations of his sensory defect. If we lose sight of this principle are we not sometimes in danger of teaching speech with too much intensity?'

> An 11-year-old severely deaf girl was referred at the request of her parents. She was attending a school which adopted an oral/auditory approach to communication. She was having speech training at school and insisted on attempting to speak. However, her attempts to do so resulted in sounds which were not only unintelligible but bizarre and a source of embarrassment to all the family. Indeed, the girl's father kept her in her bedroom whenever there were visitors and refused to accompany her outside their home. The family had agreed that the only possible solution was to seek help in the hope of finding someone who would recommend surgery to paralyse her vocal chords.

The education of deaf children is further complicated by the fact that the degree of deafness does not always remain static. It may improve but it often deteriorates. It may even vary from time to time. Moreover, many other factors need to be taken into consideration. It is obvious that the decision as to the method of communication to be employed is a complex and difficult one and should not be made on the results of audiometry alone. The following factors must be considered in their assessment

Age of onset

The age of onset of deafness is crucial in terms of the development of speech and verbal language. Deafness from birth or early age will affect their development.

Some children are born deaf. Those who are born normally hearing can become deaf at any age. Children who are born deaf, or become deaf before speech and language are acquired, have a sensory deficit. Those who become deaf after speech and language have developed suffer a sensory deprivation.

Degree of deafness

Deafness can be of any degree from a partial loss in one ear to bilateral profound deafness. Deafness may be progressive or static. It may vary from time to time.

Much confusion has arisen over the term 'profound'. It should be used to describe deafness of such a degree that the child is unable to understand speech even with amplification (see Appendix One).

> A deaf child was referred by a consultant child psychiatrist and it was decided that the examination would take place in his school. The school adopted a purely oral approach to communication and the headmaster was a militant advocate of that approach.

> After the child had been examined the author and the headmaster met in the latter's office and the question of methodology inevitably arose. After some discussion the headmaster said that he had a preverbally profoundly deaf boy of eleven years who had good speech and language. The author expressed his disbelief. The boy was sent for. He wore a binaural hearing aid and there was no barrier to communication. He understood everything that was said and his speech was quite intelligible. 'There you are!' exclaimed the headmaster triumphantly. 'But he is not profoundly deaf,' protested the author, whereupon the headmaster produced an audiogram which showed a profound loss over most frequencies. The author then asked the boy to face the wall.

He could still hear and understand everything that was said without seeing the speaker!

Deaf children with disabilities

Some deaf children have disabilities which make their education more difficult. Normal deaf children will be able to cope more easily than children who are mentally impaired. Preverbally profoundly deaf children who have relatively minor degrees of impairment will have considerable difficulty in acquiring functional literacy in English.

Visual and motor difficulties are also not uncommon and some deaf children have specific language disorders (see p.42). Visual difficulties will interfere with the reception of communication, and motor difficulties may affect the ability of some children to express themselves using sign language. Specific language disorders will affect language development globally (see Appendix One). It is important that deaf children with Usher's syndrome are recognised as early as possible because it is vitally important that every effort is made to give them functional literacy.

The family

Parents are the most potent force in any child's development. A deaf child may be the only deaf member of the family or there may be others who are deaf also. Deaf children of deaf parents are usually exposed to sign language from early life. If the child is profoundly deaf this will be to his advantage as he will acquire his first language naturally and from the beginning. Some deaf children who have deaf parents have useful hearing for speech with amplification. It is important that this is recognised and that these children are given the opportunity to acquire oral/auditory skills as well as sign language from an early age.

Even today, some hearing parents of deaf children are actively discouraged from learning sign language and so are unable to communicate effectively with their children in the early formative years. Sadly, the parents of some deaf children are still given unrealistic and over-optimistic advice and are led to believe that their children will acquire good verbal language and oral skills which will enable them to integrate into hearing society (Denmark et al. 1979). This can have devastating consequences, either leading to feelings of guilt and overprotection or to overt rejection. Marital and other family problems not uncommonly result (Denmark 1973). Some parents, unaware of the psychological and sociological implications of deafness, at first accept such guidance but eventually come to appreciate the reality of the situation. Lee Katz, one-time Executive Director of the International Association of Parents of the Deaf, in a letter written to the author in 1973 wrote:

> Fred Schreiber* slid a copy of Hearing across my desk suggesting that your article, 'The Education of Deaf Children', was well worth reading. I am grateful to him for having done so and I want to commend you on the overview you so skillfully presented.
>
> Parents we know who have been the familiar steps of (1) oralism, (2) failure, and (3) 'Oh my God why didn't someone tell me before', often make certain claims after their child is older. They say they would have been willing and anxious to develop new modes of communication – sign language – in the very beginning if only the need had been presented to them. Parents state that while it may have been true that many of their questions at the start revolved around the acquisition of speech, lipreading and going to a normal school; that it was encumbent upon professionals to enlighten them at this point in time, not join them in perpetuating an impossible dream.
>
> It was of particular interest to read your statement: 'There is a strong case for teachers of the deaf to undertake periods of teaching in normal schools'. Bravo! May I add to that that there is also a need for teachers to spend a week or so, in homes of families of their students. This could help them to better understand the need families have along with those of the child who is deaf. This experience might possibly add the ingredient of reality to advice on management of the deaf child in the home.

Another mother of a deaf child (Taylor 1988, personal communication) wrote:

> I have a son, Scott, who was born profoundly deaf four years ago. As he is an extremely intelligent child I have become concerned over his education and have for the past 6 months trying to get our local education authority to agree that an oral education will not and cannot work for him. I took it upon myself to learn BSL as I had no way of communicating with him. This he picked up readily and easily and uses it all the time. When it came to the time for him to start nursery we came to a compromise and allowed him to go to a local school with a unit for the deaf on the understanding that the staff there would learn BSL. After 12 months it was apparent that the amount of sign language needed was not available and

---

*   One-time Executive Director of the National Association of the Deaf, USA.

that signs were only used for signed assisted English. This I feel is not enough to enable them to actually teach him at school level. I went to see how things worked elsewhere and was delighted to see that all the children were learning by manual and oral communication and how well this was working especially as they had the added assistance of deaf instructors. I then applied for my son's transfer to this school but was turned down. We now intend to appeal against this decision as this is such a critical time in my son's life. Would it be possible for you to write a short statement confirming my beliefs and in support of my appeal? This letter is written in desperation as I do not want my son to be another victim of a totally oral education, because at the moment he is a very happy well adjusted little boy and I intend for him to remain that way.

Four years later the same mother wrote:

I wrote to you when we were fighting our Local Education Authority for Scott to go to a school in Leeds where they use BSL when teaching the deaf. To be honest I cannot remember what I wrote in that letter. It was written out of sheer desperation at the time because after I had read a paper you had written on the education of deaf children I knew you understood how I felt and at that time I was looking for help to further my case for Scott to be taught by sign language.

Four years ago Scott's future I thought was hanging in the balance. I knew that he would not and could not receive the education I knew he was capable of within an oral education system. He was becoming disruptive at school and I felt he was developing behaviour problems, mostly, I felt through boredom and other people's lack of understanding. Those days were, I still feel now, the blackest days I have ever had to go through.

What a different story it is four years on. I now have a lovely, lively eight-year-old whose zest for life and understanding of it is the envy of everyone. He attends Cottingley Primary School in Leeds, where he is in a mainstream school with help from a teacher of the deaf, plus a 'deaf instructor' who is deaf herself. The teacher of the deaf teaches mainly English and the 'deaf instructor' teaches them mainly communication skills using BSL. All the staff and children throughout the school have an understanding of the deaf children's needs. Last year when he was seven he had to be tested because of the new STATS the government brought out. His results were extremely good and compared favourably with his hearing peers.

The oralists who believe that sign language impairs speech and makes a child lazy and not want to use speech should see Scott. He is, in his own time learning to speak beautifully and his lipreading is wonderful.

Preverbally profoundly deaf children need a 'bilingual' approach. Sign language will be their first language and English their second one. Their preverbal stage is a long one but, provided they are given the proper help, they will be able to communicate effectively in sign language. Later, many will become fluent in English. Some will be competent lipreaders, but nearly all will experience difficulties in communicating with hearing people because of their poor speech.

Some deaf children with useful hearing for speech with amplification will be able to communicate using oral/auditory methods and English will be their first language. Many of these children will not experience major communication problems when all the conditions are right, in other words, when face-to-face, in good light and when clear speech is used. Many will learn to speak intelligibly and become good lipreaders. However, many will experience difficulties in understanding and being understood in less than ideal conditions. They, too, can benefit from the use of sign language. Many schools now accept that sign language can help to clarify meaning and use what is termed 'Signs Supporting English'.

Many deaf children who are educated using oral/auditory methods may cope reasonably well at school but afterwards find difficulties in integrating into hearing society. They find that their speech is often not fully understood and that they have difficulty in understanding in less than ideal conditions. Communication is often difficult, frustrating and tiring. Many find their solace in joining societies for deaf people who communicate by sign language.

Deaf children are very heterogeneous. Their deafness varies and so do their personalities and intelligence. Some have other disabilities. They have different backgrounds. Their assessment may be very difficult and the prescription for management will often vary from child to child. In particular, the method(s) of communication must suit the child rather than the child suit the method. Moreover, every deaf child should be reassessed at regular intervals.

There have been major changes in the education of deaf children in the last two decades. An improved understanding of the psycho-social aspects of deafness has led to an appreciation of the need for the early use of sign language for many deaf children. Two decades ago the National College of Teachers of the Deaf (now the British Association of Teachers of the Deaf) adopted an aural/oral approach to teaching and did not accept that deaf teachers had a part to play. However, most teachers now accept the fallacy of these views.

Recent years have also seen the demise of most residential schools for deaf children. The development of units for deaf children in regular schools began this process and the Warnock Committee of Enquity into the Education of Handicapped Children and Young people (1978), which recommended that children with disabilities should be integrated into mainstream education, accelerated it.

There are, of course, advantages to having units for deaf children in regular schools. Children can remain at home and can mix with hearing children to the mutual benefit of both. However, there are disadvantages. Deaf children in rural communities may have limited access to their deaf peers and will not have the opportunity to learn about and become part of the deaf culture. In many areas, teachers of deaf children do not have the communication skills appropriate to their work. The education of deaf children will remain a complex and difficult field for some time to come.

CHILDREN OF DEAF PARENTS

Children of deaf parents may be deaf or hearing.

Deaf children of deaf parents

Most, but not all, deaf people choose deaf partners and their children may also be deaf. Most deaf children of deaf parents are profoundly deaf. However, they may be partially deaf and have useful hearing for speech, with or without amplification. It is important that any useful hearing for speech is recognised early, that hearing aids are prescribed and, if both their parents are without speech, that children are given adequate exposure to speech.

Most profoundly deaf children of deaf parents will have the advantage of developing their natural language, sign language, right from the start, in the vital early formative years. In contrast to many deaf children of hearing parents, they are fully integrated, active members of the family. It is not surprising that deaf children of deaf parents are invariably more emotionally stable and more sociable than most deaf children with hearing parents. Moreover, their command of English and scholastic achievements are better than deaf children of hearing parents.

Hearing children of deaf parents

Approximately 90% of children of deaf parents have normal hearing. Deaf parents with hearing children often rely upon them to answer the door or the telephone, although with advances in technology there are now visual aids which are gradually eliminating this need. If deaf parents have limited lipreading skills or poor speech, their hearing children often interpret for them. Some hearing children of deaf parents, because of their insights in the implications of deafness and their skills in sign language, choose to work with deaf people.

Some hearing children believe that there are disadvantages in having deaf parents. They feel that the responsibilities that they have to bear in interpreting and explaining on behalf of their parents are often difficult and onerous. The topics which they have to interpret or explain are oten of a serious nature and ones with which children are not usually conversant. Some children who have deaf parents feel that they have been deprived of their childhood.

Some hearing children who have deaf parents are proud of them, but others experience embarrassment because they are unable to speak. They may develop feelings of bitterness if their parents are the objects of derision of other children.

Workers with deaf people need to be aware of the possible problems faced by hearing children of deaf parents and social workers with deaf people should accept that this is an area in which ongoing support and counselling may be necessary.

POST-LINGUAL DEAFNESS

'My experiences are naturally different from those who are born deaf because I have made the bleak journey from the world of the hearing to the world of silence. The born deaf are denied the advantages gained by the deafened before their hearing loss. I had enjoyed the natural acquisition of speech and language and had a knowledge of the hearing world. These are priceless assets in attempting to cope with total deafness. But I am painfully aware of what I have lost. My perception of that loss is a lifelong burden.' (Lord Ashley 1973)

Deafness with onset after the development of speech and verbal language is termed 'post-lingual' deafness. Other terms include 'acquired' and 'adventitious' deafness. Post-lingual deafness is usually of gradual onset and begins in one ear. However, the rate of development varies and bilateral profound deafness of sudden onset is not uncommon. The effects of post-lingual deafness depend not only on the rate of onset and the degree of deafness but also upon the intelligence, personality and life-style, in other words, the culture, marital and family status, occupation and interests, of the affected person.

The most obvious handicap of deafened people is that they can no longer hear the spoken word easily, or not at all. They not only have difficulty in one-to-one conversation but are unable to overhear the conversation of others. They can no longer determine the tone of voice which can convey so much meaning.

Inability to hear the door-bell or the telephone, to listen to the radio or follow the dialogue on television adds to the feelings of isolation. Deafened people no longer feel a part of things. Hearing contributes to our aesthetic experiences in varying degrees and for some the inability to hear music and the sounds of nature is a serious loss. Beethoven (1802) wrote 'There can be no relaxation in human society, no refined conversation, no mutual confidences. I must live alone and may creep into society only as often as sheer necessity demands. I must live like an outcast.'

Hearing is the channel through which we receive signals and warnings of events outside our field of vision and in darkness. Through hearing we monitor our speech and control its volume and pitch. In spite of speech therapy, many deafened people find that their speech deteriorates.

Deafness may affect the person's whole life-style. A deafened person with an occupation which depends upon hearing, such as a telephonist or a musician, may have to find an alternative vocation. The communication problems may cause embarrassment, especially in relationships with the opposite sex. The extrovert will find the difficulties in interpersonal communication a greater burden than the introvert. Even deaf people with good lipreading ability find the concentration stressful and tiring. Illiterate deaf people may find communication a tremendous problem.

The commonest feelings of deafened people are those of isolation, frustration, insecurity and depression. Depression, especially when the deafness is of acute or subacute onset, can be severe. Lehmann (1954) described the acute onset of depression as 'one of life's most terrifying experiences' while Levine (1960) wrote 'The abruptly deafened adult experiences in one highly concentrated measure all the pangs and agonies of years of progressive deafness'.

The greatest problem facing deafened people is adjustment to their loss. Sadly, access to rehabilitation services is extremely limited. Link, a rehabilitation facility in Eastbourne, and that in Birmingham are oases of help. The help afforded deafened people contrasts starkly with the wealth of services for people who lose their sight.

Post-lingual deafness not only affects the individual but the whole family also. Not only, therefore, should the deafened person be afforded support but the family also.

Mrs B was referred by her general practitioner. He wrote:

> This is a lady with profound deafness who has been exhaustively investigated by a professor of audiology, a neurologist and an ear, nose and throat surgeon. Her audiogram showed profound deafness but no organic cause could be found to explain this. My personal opinion is that there is a psychiatric reason. Arrangements have been made for her to attend the Deaf Society, feeling that withdrawal is the greatest single factor in her depression. I would be grateful if you would see her at one of your clinics in Manchester.

The neurologist reported that Mrs B had been quite well until about two years previously when she noticed that she was becoming deaf, and that her mother was deaf before she died at the age of 32. The Professor of Audiology had commented 'The results of testing suggest her hearing loss is entirely organic, the exact nature of which is uncertain. There is little further we can do for her'.

Mrs B was profoundly deaf and had poor lipreading ability. However, she gave a good account and communication was facilitated when necessary by writing. She said that she was anxious, depressed and wept easily, that she had seen a number of specialists but that no-one had offered her any help or advice. She was anxious in case she did not express herself well and had brought some written notes. She had written:

> At times I feel I must be going out of my mind with frustration not knowing what is going on around me and I know I am making other people miserable as well with my constant tears. I wish I could do something about it. How do other people cope I keep asking myself. I cannot go and have a chat like other people do or lift the phone or anything else a hearing person does to get over bad moods. It is hard to believe in a time of heart and kidney transplants, and even getting ahead in cancer research, there is nothing that can be done for deafness. Even more frustrating, I would like to know why I went deaf in the first place.

Mrs B explained that at first she did not know that she was going deaf but that it had been brought to her notice by a neighbour who thought that she had ignored her knocking at her door. Her hearing had thereafter gradually got worse over twelve months until she had become completely deaf. Of all the consequences of her deafness the one that most upset her was that her children no longer approached her as she could not understand what they were saying.

Mrs B was overtly depressed. However there were no features of a biological affective disorder and it seemed that all her problems were related to her deafness. After discussion it was decided to refer her to 'Link', a rehabilitation centre for deafened people (see Appendix Three). Both Mrs B and her husband attended a residential course there where they received counselling and guidance. After her return home she wrote,

> The course has done me the world of good. It has given me back the will to live. I was horribly depressed and the thought of spending a lifetime of deafness horrified me. Now I can see I can live a very near normal life and things are not as black as they once were.

Many deafened people suffer in silence and loneliness because they do not have a sense of identity with those who suffer similarly. Unfortunately, it is assumed that because they have speech they can access non-specialist mental health services. However, they are often misunderstood by workers who are without an appreciation of the psycho-social implications of post-lingual deafness.

In the United Kingdom people who are deafened in adult life rarely identify with the preverbally deaf community who use British Sign Language. The vast majority of them 'hang on' to their hearing identity and develop sophisticated coping mechanisms. However, communication between many deafened and hearing people is often nothing but a sham.

JB, aged 36, was referred by the medical officer of a remand centre. He had been charged with assault on a police officer. He had been married for 12 years and had two young children. He had worked as a fitter and life had presented no major problems until some two years previously when he had become profoundly deaf in both ears following a road traffic accident.

J had become very depressed. He was seen by an otologist but had been offered no help. He had merely been told that his deafness was permanent and that hearing aids would be of no use. He found great difficulty in understanding everybody, even his own family. He had to give up his job and he became depressed and irritable. Marital difficulties ensued.

Some three months after his accident J made a serious attempt at suicide and was admitted to a mental hospital. Surprisingly, he was treated with electro-convulsive therapy, but not surprisingly he derived no benefit. He took his discharge. He did not return home but went into lodgings.

J gradually became a recluse and often befriended stray cats. One day, while on his way down a narrow passage to a derelict house to take scraps of food to some cats, he was frightened by someone roughly taking hold of him from behind. He had not, of course, heard their approach and responded by turning quickly and raising his hand. His 'assailant' was a policeman and in turning he had knocked off his helmet.

History taking and examination proved to be difficult and prolonged as J was a poor lip-reader. However, there was no evidence of mental disorder and his behaviour was not an assault but fully comprehensible in the circumstances.

A psychiatric report was made and the case was dismissed.

Deafness should always be investigated, for it may be treatable and it can often be helped by aids to hearing. Support and guidance both for the subject and the family can alleviate much distress and help adjustment. Depressive reactions to post-lingual deafness are understandable. However, when depression is severe or protracted other causes should be considered.

The British Association of the Hard of Hearing was founded to provide support for deafened people. It is of interest that many of its members are profoundly deaf. The distinction between the preverbally deaf who use sign language and whose parent body is the British Deaf Association, and those who are deafened post-lingually and who do not use sign language and belong to the British Association for the Hard of Hearing, is not so apparent in the USA. There people who have all types of deafness have one national body, the National Association of the Deaf.

CHAPTER TWO

THOSE WHO ARE BOTH
DEAF AND BLIND

Both hearing and vision are important in communication but the role of visual clues is sometimes not fully understood. The importance of facial, expression, body language and 'unconscious' lipreading are illustrated in the following anecdote.

At the age of 14 years, the author spent a week-end camping with two pupils from his father's school. One was profoundly deaf in one ear but had useful hearing for speech with the help of a hearing aid in the other. He had good verbal language, his speech was intelligible and he was a good lipreader. He was also fluent in sign language and in fingerspelling. The second boy was profoundly deaf. He was without speech. His English language was limited and so his ability to lipread and to fingerspell was poor. He, too, was fluent in sign language.

Communication between the three boys usually presented no problems. However, as the days drew to a close and the light failed the situation became quite different. Both the author and his partially deaf friend found it impossible to communicate with their profoundly deaf friend, for not only could he not see or hear but, because of his limited English language, it was impossible to communicate with him by touch – by 'writing' with a finger on the palm of his hand. (At that time neither the author nor his friend were aware of the deaf/blind manual alphabet.) To communicate with him it was necessary to use an electric torch.

Communication between the author and his partially deaf friend also presented problems when the light was poor. Whereas the speech of the latter was easily understood while the light was good, it was not so easily understood in the dark. Similarly, although he appeared to have good hearing for speech when the conditions were right, he experienced considerable difficulty in understanding in the dark. However, they were able to communicate by touch by 'writing' on the palms of the hands.

Deafness and blindness are usually single disabilities, but they may co-exist. Moreover, the incidence of persons affected by both disabilities is far greater than would be expected if the relationship was coincidental. The reason for this is that the two disabilities can be caused by the same noxious agents such as the rubella virus affecting the foetus if the mother is infected in the first trimester of pregnancy, or they may occur together as part inherited syndromes such as Usher's syndrome (Usher 1914). The true incidence of people affected by the two disabilities is difficult to determine. In 1968 the Department of Social Security identified 1648 people registered as both deaf and blind. However this figure included only those who were both profoundly deaf and totally blind. If those with lesser degrees of deafness and those who are partially sighted are included then the numbers must be very much higher.

The effects of deafness and visual impairment depend upon the different degrees and ages of onset of the two disabilities but also upon the individual affected. Some people who are both deaf and blind live independently but others do not. It is impossible to describe the wide variety of different pictures presented. However, broad groupings can be described.

Both deafness and visual impairments interfere with communication and this section will focus upon the problems presented from this point of view. Moreover, the comments will focus on those persons who are profoundly deaf and who have no sight – the deaf/blind.

There are four broad groups of people who are both deaf and blind:

Deaf/blind people who are born normally sighted and with normal hearing

People who are born with normal sight and hearing may become both deaf and blind at any age. Deafness and blindness may occur at the same time or one may precede the other. People who become deaf and blind in adolescence or in adult life will be able to speak and, unless they are illiterate, will be able to learn to receive communication by the deaf/blind manual alphabet (see Figure 4) or by 'block writing' on the palm of the hand. They will also be able to learn to read Braille and Moon (see Glossary). Illiterate people who become deaf and blind will have great difficulty in understanding others.

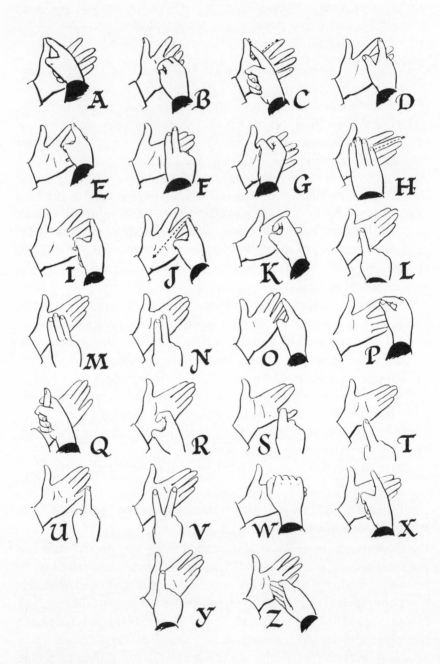

Figure 4 The deaf–blind manual alphabet

The effects of both deafness and blindness will depend not only on the age of onset and their degree but also upon the individual affected. Intelligence is of particular importance. If those who are both deaf and blind and also have an intellectual disability severe enough to preclude literacy, then there will be immense problems in communicating, for they will be unable to use the deaf/blind manual alphabet (see Figure 4) or read braille. Moreover, the speech of some people, particularly those with sensorineural deafness, may deteriorate because of difficulty in monitoring their own voices.

The loss of both sight and hearing can be extremely traumatic experiences.

JD, a 24-year-old woman, was referred by a psychiatrist, with a history of overtly disturbed behaviour. She had become both deaf and blind and had been admitted to a mental hospital. She was described as 'noisy, abusive, given to using foul language, removing her clothing and masturbating in front of others'.

J was born with normal hearing and sight. She had always been regarded as having an mild degree of mental impairment. At the age of 16 she became difficult to manage and was admitted to a hostel for young people. Her behaviour improved and she married. However, the marriage failed and she eventually returned to her parents' home.

At the age of 22, J was involved in a road traffic accident but did not suffer any serious injury. A year later she began to complain of dizziness and deafness. Her general practitioner treated her with analgesics. Her symptoms continued and she also complained of poor vision. She was eventually diagnosed as having bilateral acoustic neromas. (Innocent tumours of the sheath of the eighth cranial nerve.) These were satisfactorily removed but by that time she was totally deaf in both ears and totally blind. She had become so disturbed that she had been admitted to a mental hospital where she was treated with both anxiolytic and major tranquillising drugs. She was then discharged to a hostel.

J was an obese young woman. She had oral dyskinesia and akathisia of the legs, almost certainly due to treatment with neuroleptic medication. There was a left facial paresis.

Communication proved to be very difficult. She spoke in a loud voice but her speech was slurred and difficult to follow, probably due to medication. To communicate with her it was necessary to 'write' with a finger on the palm of her hand, using simple language. She showed no evidence of psychosis. Her emotional and behaviour problems appeared to be due to her sensory deprivation.

J was admitted informally. Her medication was reduced and she received a considerably amount of individual help. However, she could not be persuaded to become involved in any occupational therapeutic programmes.

Although J improved to some extent, she continued to be disturbed and she was transferred back to her parent hospital. Eventually her physical condition deteriorated and she died from bronchopneumonia.

Those who are born blind who subsequently become deaf

Those who are blind from birth will develop speech and language normally through hearing. Should they subsequently lose their hearing they will still be able to speak and, if literate, will be able to use the deaf/blind manual alphabet and learn to read Braille and Moon. Their speech may, however, deteriorate. Those who are not literate will have considerable communication difficulties.

Those who are born deaf who subsequently become blind

Few, if any, preverbally profoundly deaf people learn to speak intelligibly and some have poor verbal language. Should they become blind, their ability to use the deaf/blind manual alphabet will depend upon their level of literacy. Preverbally profoundly deaf people who have limited verbal language will be able to express themselves by sign language but they will have immense difficulties in receiving communication. Not surprisingly, emotional problems often occur.

> JP. A telephone enquiry was received from a consultant psychiatrist asking for advice about a 54-year-old deaf and blind man who had been admitted to a medical ward of a general hospital with a chest infection. It was reported that he suffered from hypertension and diabetes, that it was difficult to communicate with him, that he had become agitated and unco-operative, was refusing food and that his general condition was deteriorating. The psychiatrist thought that he might be suffering from a depressive illness and advice was sought as to whether or not he should be treated with electro-convulsive therapy.
>
> J was seen the following day, but prior to the examination his wife his son and his social worker were interviewed. His wife was profoundly

deaf and had limited verbal language but their son was normally hearing. The following history was obtained.

J was presumed to have been born deaf, although the diagnosis was not made until he was three years old. There was no family history of deafness. He began school at the age of five years, remaining until he was sixteen. On leaving school he had very limited language.

On leaving school, J worked for a short time as a joiner for an undertaker but left to join a building firm and worked as a labourer, remaining there for the rest of his working life. At the age of 26 he married a young preverbally deaf woman whom he had known at school. They had a son and a daughter who were both normally hearing.

J was described as a short-tempered man, but family life had been reasonably happy. He was said to be a good joiner. He had made a large yacht for his son when he was a boy and a doll's house for his daughter. He also made some items of furniture which were of high standard. He and his wife socialised with the local deaf community.

J's eyesight began to fail in his early thirties and at the age of 44 years he was dismissed from work.

Prior to the onset of his visual problems, communication presented no difficulty at home, for all the family used sign language. However, as his sight became worse J had difficulty in understanding even his own family, for he was functionally illiterate. He could express himself by sign language but could not understand anyone, because he could not use the deaf/blind manual alphabet. He became irritable and depressed. He over-ate and put on excessive weight.

At the age of 43, J collapsed and was admitted to hospital, where he was found to have diabetes. He was prescribed a diet and medication and discharged. Later he was found to be hypertensive also and prescribed additional medication.

In the 12 months prior to his recent admission J had become progressively more agitated and depressed. He often banged on furniture with his fists and sometimes wept. Help was sought from the local community nurse but communication proved too difficult. When proferred his medication he often refused it or threw it away.

J was an obese man. He was profoundly deaf and blind and communication proved extremely difficult. Attempts were made to communicate with him using the deaf/blind manual alphabet but with little success. It was, however, possible by using touch, to tell him that he was with a doctor, whereupon he became animated and repeatedly made the sign for 'home'.

Discussion with J's wife and son revealed that he had never understood that he had diabetes and hypertension and that when he had developed his chest infection it had not been possible to tell him that he was being admitted to hospital.

J's depression and agitation seemed comprehensible. It was suggested that he should be sent home and treated there, that his medication should be reduced to a minimum and that he should be given diabetic foods. He was immediately discharged and some few months later his social worker reported 'a tremendous improvement'.

There are a number of inherited syndromes which include both hearing and visual disabilities. The commonest of these is Usher's syndrome (see Appendix One) There are also a number of inherited syndromes which include deafness and optic atrophy. It is essential that syndromes which include deafness and visual impairments are detected as early as possible so that every effort can be made to enable affected children to acquire effective communication skills and if possible achieve functional literacy. The first language of preverbally profoundly deaf children is sign language and to deny them their right to learn it can have tragic consequences.

Those who are born both deaf and blind

Some children are born with both hearing and visual difficulties. These are of varying degrees and their education must utilise to the full any residuum of these senses. Some children are, however, born without sight or hearing. These are the two senses which are important in communication and are those through which normal children learn about the world in which they live. It is impossible for people with normal sight and hearing to put themselves in the position of children who are born without either sense and who are left to explore their environment by touch, smell and taste alone.

The teaching of children who are born both deaf and blind is extremely demanding even if there are no other disabilities. It requires both dedication and patience in the extreme.

CHAPTER THREE

CHILDREN WHO DO NOT SPEAK

INTRODUCTION

The rate at which children learn to speak varies considerably. Most children have some understanding of speech by the age of 12 months and can say a few words by 18 months. However, some children never learn to speak and there may be a number of reasons for this. Deafness is but one cause and may be difficult to differentiate from others. It may occur alone or may be accompanied by other disabilities.

The management of children suffering from different conditions may vary. It is important, therefore, that workers with deaf children are aware of the possible reasons why children fail to talk. This issue was highlighted in 1975 when the Department of Health and Social Security Advisory Committee on Services for the Hearing Impaired set up a subcommittee to consider specific matters for hearing impaired children (DSS 1981). The report commented on the 'general low level of medical training and knowledge in the developmental aspects of spoken language' and expressed concern that 'paediatricians do not take more interest in learning disorders'.

The cause of failure to speak may be obvious, such as when children have cerebral palsy, and the assessment of other children may be relatively easy. The history will often point to the cause and tests such as audiometry will often confirm the diagnosis. However, non-speaking children often have other disabilities and so do not always fall into neat diagnostic categories. In other cases there are associated behaviour problems which may cloud the clinical picture. To assess these children, special training and wide experience is necessary, including a knowledge of developmental paediatrics and neuro-psychiatry. Moreover, the examination of children with developmental disorders of communication will be greatly facilitated if workers are able to use sign language.

With the onset of adolescence and increasing sexual awareness, any behaviour problems of children with communication disorders often increase and become difficult to manage. Moreover, the exact nature of developmental disorders of communication may be difficult to determine not only in childhood but even into adult life. Patients with developmental disorders of communication are not uncommonly referred to psychiatrists who work with deaf patients and who are able to communicate by sign language. Of a series of 250 patients referred to the author (Denmark 1985), 48 (19%) had no effective means of communication. Some were deaf and had other disabilities, while others were not deaf but had developmental disorders of communication of other aetiology. It is important, therefore, that psychiatrists working with deaf people have an understanding of the reasons why children fail to learn to speak.

CAUSES OF FAILURE TO SPEAK

The normal development of spoken language depends upon: (a) exposure to the spoken word, (b) ability to hear the spoken word, (c) attention to the spoken word, (d) ability to understand the meaning of speech, and (e) ability to express thoughts in speech. Spoken language will fail to develop normally if there is delay or failure of any of the first four factors. In the case of the fifth, verbal language will develop normally but affected children will be unable to express themselves in speech.

Lack of exposure to the spoken word

This is a rare cause of failure to speak. Instances have been recorded of children who have been reared without human contact. One such case was that of a child in France who was raised by wolves in a forest until he was about ten years old (Lane 1976). In another, the author was asked to examine a non-communicating child who was brought up by his psychotic mother in a hen hutch.

Deafness

Deafness is, next to mental impairment, the commonest cause of failure to speak. It is important, therefore, that children who fail to speak are screened for hearing impairment and that they receive appropriate help. Failure to provide this help can have disastrous consequences.

GI was remanded to prison having been committed to the Crown Court on ten charges including indecent assault and buggery involving children between the ages of ten and fifteen years.

G was born deaf in 1940. According to his mother, the local school would not accept him and he received no education until a place was found for him in a school for deaf children at the age of ten years. The school adopted a purely oral approach to communication and on leaving school G had no speech or verbal language and communicated in a very limited way by gesture and pointing.

After leaving school, G had no contact with deaf people and never attended a club for the deaf. Nevertheless, he found a job on a local farm and learned to drive a tractor. He bought his own boat and enjoyed sea-fishing, gardening and helping in the local garage. He was described as placid by nature and had never previously been in trouble with the authorities. On one occasion he had saved a man from drowning.

G was seen in prison. On examination, he was without speech. He had a black eye and indicated that someone had punched him. He had some hearing in one ear but was unable to understand speech through hearing, nor did he have any lipreading ability. His communication was limited to gesture with a few signs. He could read and write a few words but was illiterate.

Psychiatric examination proved extremely difficult because of the communication problems. However, G presented as a pleasant man who cooperated fully. All methods of communication had to be tried including writing, drawing, gesture and mime. G could read and fingerspell his name and knew his age. He knew the day and month of his birth but did not know the year. He knew the number of his house but did not know the name of the street or the town in which he lived. He did not appear to know the days of the week or the months of the year. He did not know the date. He indicated that he lived with four others but was unable to give their names. His numerical ability was limited to simple addition and subtraction but he could manipulate money.

Psychological testing indicated that G was of average intelligence and it seemed that his poor communication was due to lack of appropriate help and education. Conceivably, had he been assessed audiologically and been given a hearing aid, he might have developed verbal language through hearing and even learned to speak. It is of interest that G had been examined earlier by a psychologist with the help of an interpreter and was reported to have answered a number of complex questions. However, when the same questions were put to him again, it was apparent that, although he nodded his head, he did not understand. Arrangements were made to review the transcript of the questions and answers with the interpreter who agreed that G could not have understood the questions.

G was found unfit to plead and eventually admitted to the Department of Psychiatry for the Deaf at Whittingham hospital. He was involved in individual, group and occupational therapy and communication and educational programmes and quickly acquired skills in sign language. After nearly two years he was transferred to a rehabilitation facility for deaf people where he made further progress. G is now married, has his own home and works full time as a gardener/handyman.

In recent years there has been a marked increase in the number of immigrants, many of them coming from under-developed countries. Among these have been deaf people of all ages. Some have hearing which, with amplification, would have enabled them to hear and understand speech. However, many have not been assessed audiometrically and hearing aids have not been prescribed. Others are preverbally profoundly deaf and have not received any special education.

Lack of attention to the spoken word

Some children do not attend to speech because they are intellectually impaired, while others are mentally ill.

Mental impairment

Mental impairment is the commonest single cause of failure to develop speech and it is for this reason that the word 'dumb' is often used colloquially with this meaning.

Language is intimately related to intelligence. Mentally impaired children develop spoken language more slowly than children of normal intelligence. Severe impairment may result in complete failure to learn to speak. In such cases overall delayed development is the rule and other features are usually present also. Mental impairment can, of cause, be associated with other disabilities.

Mental illness

Mental illness can occur in childhood. The older children are when they becomes mentally ill, the more closely do the clinical features resemble those of the adult. However, very young children cannot exhibit symptomatology with all the features of the adult for they do not have the sophistication of language to express their experiences and feelings. The presentation is, consequently, in the child's behaviour.

Childhood psychosis dating from the early years has been termed 'infantile autism' (Kanner 1943). It is characterised by withdrawal and impairment of emotional relationships. Autistic children dislike being touched and avoid eye contact. Stereotyped manneristic behaviour occurs and there is often preoccupation with certain objects. Obsessional preoccupation and dislike of change are common. Anxiety and self injury may occur without apparent cause. Some children fail to develop speech while others start to speak and then stop. Autistic children are sometimes mistakenly thought to be deaf and *vice versa*.

Deafness and autism may coexist. In a study of 250 patients referred to the author, 48 had severe communication problems and of these four were both deaf and autistic (Denmark 1985). Unfortunately, and not uncommonly, one disability may mask the presence of another.

> PB was referred at the age of 11 years by the headmaster of a school for deaf children because of her inability to communicate and her strange behaviour. Unfortunately, little was known of her early history other than that she had never learned to speak and had always been a strange child. She had been hospitalised on at least two occasions for investigation and assessment and there was no doubt that she was profoundly deaf. The results of psychological assessment indicated that she was not unintelligent. However, deafness was not her only problem for attempts had been made to get her to communicate using a variety of methods including Makaton without any success.

> P was seen with her teacher, who reported that she used a few signs but that these tended to be repeated in a stereotyped manner. Her teacher thought that she had a greater receptive vocabulary. She was solitary and rarely made any attempt to communicate with either other pupils or staff. She would not interact in any way with the other children but played by herself for long periods. She disliked change and when asked to do simple tasks would react by kicking, banging her head on a table or biting herself. She would do this for from ten to thirty minutes at a time.

Physically, P appeared to be a normal child. However, she took no interest in her surroundings but sat on the floor completely self-absorbed. Attempts to make contact with her were to no avail. Later she was observed in the playground. Again, she took no notice of the other children but, until interrupted at the end of playtime, repeatedly picked up handfuls of fallen leaves then threw them into the air.

Inability to understand the meaning of speech

Some children who do not speak can hear normally, are not unintelligent, are not mentally ill and do not have any apparent disorder of physiology or anatomy which would affect the expression of verbal language through speech. The reason they cannot speak is because they are unable to understand verbal language. These children suffer from a disorder of language due to a lesion of the brain.

Many terms have been used to describe this condition, including 'aphasia', 'congenital auditory imperception' (Worster-Drought 1963) and 'central deafness' (Gordon 1964). However, the term 'aphasia' is best used to describe disorders which affect the production of speech, while terminology which include the words 'deafness' or 'auditory' imply that the defect pertains to the sense of hearing. If this were so, affected children would function as deaf children and would be able to learn to read and write. A better term is 'specific language disorder'. In this context, it should be noted that a preverbally profoundly deaf child with dyslexia would present as a child with a specific language disorder. However, such children could be differentiated by demonstrating that in the case of the child with a specific language disorder there is no defect of hearing. (The two disabilities can, of course, coexist.)

In its pure form, specific language disorder is relatively uncommon, but lesser degrees are probably more common than is generally thought. It may occur as a single disability, or may co-exist with others.

ET was referred at the age of 15 years by a Director of Social Services at the suggestion of a consultant child psychiatrist and with the agreement of his general practitioner.

E was the eldest of four children. His father was Portuguese and had a history of recurrent depression. He was attending a mental hospital as a day-patient.

E had been a full-term baby of 6 pounds 11 ounces who was born normally. His developmental milestones were within normal limits but he failed to speak. When he was less than twelve months old he was referred to hospital for assessment. He was difficult to test because he was 'given to bouts of screaming and kicking' and the results of hearing tests were not known. There was no family history of deafness.

At the age of four, E began attending the local school for deaf children but he made no educational progress. The teachers thought he was not deaf. On psychometric testing he achieved a performance intelligence quotient of 113.

E was reported to be unable to communicate in any medium and produced 'only imitated gestures'. He was said to draw 'with intelligence' and to be adept at modelling. However, he sometimes destroyed models before they were finished. He was prone to tantrums and was occasionally aggressive. His mother refused to allow him to stay away from home. He stopped attending school at the age of 14 years.

E presented as a somewhat overweight youth who showed no physical abnormality. He did not speak and did not respond to speech. He made good eye contact and smiled pleasantly. He appeared to want to communicate, for he kept repeating the sign for 'good'. He could write his name and had a small written vocabulary of nouns but could not understand even a very simple sentence. Attempts to communicate with him by sign language and gesture brought about echopractic responses only.

Physical examination and extensive investigations revealed no abnormality. Evoked-response electro-encephalography indicated that E had no appreciable degree of deafness and repeat psychometric testing using non-verbal tests showed him to be of average innate intellectual potential.

Inability to express thoughts in speech

There are some children who can hear and understand speech but who are unable to express themselves because of disorders of the structures or mechanisms involved in speech production. These disorders may involve (a) lesions of the cerebral motor cortex, giving rise to expressive (motor) aphasia, (b) disorders of voice production (aphonia or dysphonia), or (c) disorders of articulation (anarthria or dysarthria). There may, of course, be combinations of these disorders.

Expressive (motor) aphasia

Some workers use the term 'aphasia' to mean, or to include, inability to understand speech, but it is preferable to confine the term to mean inability to speak in the presence of normal language but not due to aphonia or anarthria. In other words the condition is an inability to express thoughts in speech due to a disorder of ideo-motor function. The lesion lies in the third left frontal convolution of the brain in right-handed people and in the third right convolution in left-handed people.

Aphonia and anarthria

Aphonia (absence of voice) and anarthria (lack of ability to articulate) usually occur together and are frequently due to cerebral palsy. Some children with serious cerebral palsy may be unable to express themselves even by gesture (apraxia). Such patients are 'locked in' and yet may be fully aware of their surroundings. Recognition of the condition is important lest casual remarks are overheard and understood by the subject, causing great distress.

> WGH was born with severe spastic quadriplegia and with generalised choreo-athetosis. He never learned to walk or talk but drew attention to himself by making strange noises. At the age of six years he was diagnosed as severely mentally retarded. His mother coped with him until he was 17 years old when he was admitted to a hospital for the mentally impaired. He required total care.
>
> W was regarded as severely mentally impaired until a member of the nursing staff suspected that he understood all that was said. He put this to the test by asking him to respond to questions by nodding his head – to nod once to indicate an affirmative answer and twice for a negative answer. It quickly became obvious that he understood everything that was said. Subsequently he was taught to read. He was provided with a typewriter and was able to express himself by depressing the keys with a peg attached to the sole of his shoe.

In recent years there have been great advances in microchip technology and there are now a large number of devices which enable people with communication disorders to communicate more effectively. Information in this respect can be obtained from the National Council for Educational Technology and Access to Communication in Education.

Elective mutism

This chapter is concerned with children who fail to learn to speak. For the sake of completeness mention should be made of children who learn to speak but do not do so in certain circumstances. The term 'elective mutism' was given to this condition (Tramer 1934). It often only becomes apparent when the child starts school. Affected children are usually anxious, often come from poor homes and may be of unprepossessing appearance.

CHAPTER FOUR

PSYCHIATRY FOR DEAF PEOPLE
CLINICAL ASPECTS

'We should try to talk to our patients in language that they can understand.' (Fletcher 1973)

INTRODUCTION

Mental disorders affect people of every class and every culture and can have devastating effects on the individual, the family and friends. While mental disorders can often be effectively treated, there can be no treatment without diagnosis, and communication is the cornerstone of diagnosis. Communication between doctor and patient is important in all branches of medicine both for diagnosis and treatment.

DB, a 42-year-old preverbally profoundly deaf man, was referred by his general practitioner, who had written the following letter:

> This man is a new patient to me. He is a deaf mute presumably due to an accident 12 years ago. He has asked me to write to you for an appointment and perhaps you would be good enough to see him at your earliest convenience. Please write directly to the patient.
>
> I am enclosing a note he brought to me.

The note was written as follows:

> Please would you help me to write to Dr at Preston, he can sign Deaf. Maybe he would help me for Deaf. I always pain back and legs I never better my body I have fell 3 up window almost 12 years ago at Glasgow.
>
> You will write to Dr. John Denmark at Preston.

It was obvious that the patient wanted to be seen by a doctor who could communicate with him by sign language. However, his general practitioner, not understanding that his lack of speech was because his deafness was preverbal, concluded that he had lost his voice because of an accident 12 years previously.

As B walked into the room, it was apparent from his gait and bodily movements that he had a rigid spine and the author suspected that he was suffering from ankylosing spondylitis.

B was without speech and communicated by finger-spelling and sign language. He was an intelligent man and gave a good account. He 'said', using sign language, that he knew that the author worked with mentally ill people but he was at pains to point out that he was not mentally ill. He had heard of the author's work from other deaf people.

B had a number of complaints. The first was of progressive difficulty in turning his body and in stooping. His second was of epigastric pain which was sometimes associated with vomiting. He reported that the vomit was often dark in colour. His third complaint was of pain on defaecation. His faeces were often bloodstained. He 'said' that he had seen a number of doctors both in England and in Scotland. He had had blood tests and X-rays but had not been informed of the results.

Examination revealed a rigid spine, epigastric tenderness and prolapsed and bleeding haemorrhoids. It was concluded that B had ankylosing spondylitis and a peptic ulcer in addition to haemorrhoids.

The author explained, using sign language, that X-rays were needed to confirm the first two diagnoses and 'said' that he would write to his general practitioner who would arrange for tests and treatment. D then commented that he felt at ease with the author because he could communicate with him. He added that he knew the author's department was for deaf people who were mentally ill but that he felt, nevertheless, that he would be happier there than in a hospital where he could not communicate with anybody.

D was admitted to hospital through the author's department where X-rays and blood tests confirmed the diagnoses. It was explained that the spondylitis was untreatable. His peptic ulcer responded well to conservative medical treatment and he was referred to a surgical colleague who removed his haemorrhoids.

This case history illustrates the importance of communication between doctor and patient in physical medicine. In psychiatry, effective communication is absolutely vital. Patients need to be able to express themselves and psychiatrists have to be able to understand them. Psychiatric diagnosis in the case of hearing patients is often easy but it may be difficult, especially when patients have a poor command of language and so do not give a good account.

Sometimes psychiatrists not only have to be able to understand what patients are thinking (their thought content), but may also find it to be important to take into account the form of their thinking. The form, that is, the manner, of thinking can be an important diagnostic feature in both affective disorder (manic-depressive illness) and in schizophrenia. In the former, the retardation of thought of depression or the pressure of thought of hypomania or mania, can be important diagnostic features. Similarly, the concrete or the paralogical thinking of schizophrenia can be important features in diagnosis. However, it is not only the content and form of thinking that are of diagnostic importance. So, also, is the emotional tone of speech. It follows that any communication barrier, however slight, between patient and psychiatrist can lead to difficulties in diagnosis.

When preverbally deaf people have both poor verbal language and poor sign language skills they will have great difficulty in describing their feelings and beliefs. In such circumstances it may be difficult, and at times impossible, to detect the presence of abnormal psychic phenomena. As a result, mental illness may remain undiagnosed. In other instances, mental illness or mental impairment may be mistakenly diagnosed. Perhaps not surprisingly, when deaf people are admitted to psychiatric hospitals they tend to remain much longer than hearing patients. In a study of the deaf population of two mental hospitals in the north west of England (Denmark 1966) they were found to be over-represented, and a study in Belgium revealed that deaf people remained in mental hospitals on average for 17 years, which was over 40 times longer than hearing people (Timmermans 1988).

The importance of communication in psychiatry is exemplified by an extract from a letter written by a consultant psychiatrist to the author. He wrote:

> *I would be grateful if you would consider assessing this 50-year-old single man for me.*
>
> *I enclose a case history which summarises what is known about his past. This hospital will close in 1991 and I have the task of planning an alternative provision for him. Any sensible approach to this task is thwarted by the fact that after over 30 years in psychiatric hospitals we still do not know what is wrong with him. In the past he has been diagnosed as being mentally handicapped and schizophrenic but I think the evidence supporting these diagnoses is very slim.*

The patient was transferred to the Department of Psychiatry for the deaf at Whittingham Hospital where it became apparent that he was of average intelligence but suffering from paranoid schizophrenia.

If mistakes in diagnosis and treatment are not to be made, deaf people must have access to special mental health services where psychiatrists and other mental health workers have the following skills and expertise:

1. Understanding of the psychological, linguistic, sociological and cultural aspects of different types of deafness.

2. Understanding of the problems of deaf children and adults with disabilities.

3. Knowledge of communication disorders, both developmental and acquired.

4. Ability to communicate with deaf people using British Sign Language, fingerspelling, the deaf/blind manual alphabet and other methods appropriate to the individual.

5. How to obtain and use specialist interpreters and relay interpreters. (British Sign Language may not be appropriate for some deaf people.)

6. Knowledge of the phenomenology of mental disorder when it affects deaf people with different types of deafness and of the pitfalls in diagnosis.

Preferably specialist mental health workers should also have should also have:

7. A working knowledge of audiological medicine including the causes, assessment, treatment and alleviation of deafness, and

8. Awareness of the services available to deaf people including aids to daily living and rehabilitation and residential facilities.

Although the greatest difficulties in diagnosis and treatment occur with preverbally deaf patients who have serious communication problems, difficulties may also occur with preverbally partially hearing patients and those who are deafened post-lingually.

J, a 14-year-old partially deaf girl, was referred by a psychiatrist at the suggestion of a social worker with deaf people. She had been admitted to a mental hospital from a residential school for partially deaf children where she had become disturbed. It transpired that the psychiatrist had at first resented the suggestion that she should be referred because she believed that all her problems related to her deafness. The psychiatrist accepted that there had been some difficulty in communication but attributed it to her deafness.

J was seen as an outpatient. She wore a binaural hearing aid. She had some hearing for speech and was a good lipreader. Her verbal language was fair and she had no difficulty in understanding speech provided that the conditions were satisfactory and clear speech and simple language were used. She expressed herself in speech but it was difficult to understand what she said. However, this was not due to her poor speech but was because she had marked thought disorder due to a schizophrenic psychosis. Although her thinking appeared to be paralogical it was possible, nevertheless, to establish that she was visually hallucinated. She said that she had seen ghosts both in school and in the hospital. They had frightened her.

J was transferred to the deaf unit and was treated with psychotropic medication. She responded well. After she had improved she related that the ghosts she had seen were men and women. She did not know them. They had spoken to her but she could not understand what they had said. She returned to school free of symptoms after three months.

THE PHENOMENOLOGY OF MENTAL DISORDER IN DEAF PEOPLE

The ways in which deaf people present when they are mentally disordered depend upon their intelligence, their personality, their background, their type of deafness, their communication methods and the type of disorder. It is important, therefore, that mental health workers have some understanding of the phenomenology of mental disorders when they affect deaf people.

Disorders of feeling

Anxiety and depression

Postlingual deafness, especially if it is of acute or subacute onset, often gives rise to feelings of anxiety and depression. However, the symptomatology is invariably suggestive of a reaction to loss. When this is not the case other causes must be considered.

Reverend A, a 65-year-old clergyman, was referred by an consultant otolaryngologist, with a history of depression. He had become progressively deaf over the previous five years and also had continuous tinnitus and bouts of vertigo. Unfortunately, he had derived no benefit from hearing aids and poor eyesight made lipreading extremely difficult. Because of his communication difficulties he had had to retire from his living.

It had been construed that A's depression was reactive in nature and efforts had been made to help him by a hearing therapist and a social worker for the deaf using both individual and group therapy but without any benefit.

When seen at an out-patient clinic the picture A presented was entirely different from that expected. He said that he felt well and he had no complaints. There was no evidence of depression. On the contrary, his mood was one of mild elation. He was garrulous and circumstantial and was difficult to interrupt. Moreover, he was quite unconcerned about his deafness or his tinnitus. Further enquiry revealed that he had had a depressive episode of unknown aetiology some years previously.

There was no doubt that A was in a hypomanic phase of a bipolar affective disorder (manic-depressive illness) and that his previous depression was in no small part unrelated to his deafness, but part of that illness. He was referred back to the psychiatrist who had treated him originally.

When depression occurs in a setting of early childhood deafness it is not usually due to the deafness itself, but results from some other cause. It has been suggested that affective disorder is less common among people with preverbal profound deafness (Altschuler 1971). Studies of referrals to special psychiatric services for deaf people appear to support this contention. However, this phenomenon is probably because few preverbally deaf people seek help, because they are not aware that depressive states are treatable and few social workers for deaf people are trained in mental health issues and so are not aware of the nature of affective disorders.

KM, a 40-year-old preverbally severely deaf man, was referred by his general practitioner at the suggestion of his social worker. She was a social worker with deaf people and was herself severely deaf.

K was profoundly deaf in one ear but had some hearing for speech with a hearing aid in his other ear. He had fair verbal language. His speech was intelligible and he was a good lipreader. However, his preferred modes of communication were sign language and fingerspelling. K's wife was also partially deaf. She, too, communicated by hearing, speech, lipreading, fingerspelling and sign language.

K had a good work record until some six months before his referral when he had fractured his ankle. He had recovered well until, quite quickly, he became depressed and restless. His employer sacked him because he thought 'he was overdoing his convalescence'.

K presented a picture of a severe depression. He could not explain why he felt so depressed. He felt worse in the morning and had terminal insomnia. He had difficulty in thinking. He had lost his appetite and had lost weight. There was also loss of libido. His social worker was unaware of the nature of affective illness.

As no bed was vacant, K was treated as an out-patient. The round trip to hospital then back home was some 50 miles. Initially, he was given a tricyclic antidepressant. However, he developed a tremor and became constipated and discontinued the medication. He was then treated with a short course of electro-convulsive therapy which brought about a complete recovery within two and a half weeks.

K remained very well for five years until he again became depressed for no apparent reason. He was again prescribed antidepressant medication. However, this brought about only a partial response for two years when he again became severely depressed and had thoughts of suicide. Fortunately, a bed was vacant and he was admitted. As he was so severely depressed and had not responded to treatment with medication, a further course of electro-convulsive treatment was commenced. To the author's surprise, this brought about no change and so he decided to witness the treatment being given. It transpired that the reason for the failure to respond was because no convulsion was being produced. Further correct treatments brought about a complete recovery.

In the subsequent two years K had two further depressive phases which responded to some extent to medication. However, he then became hypomanic with marked elevation of mood and pressure of thought amounting at times to flight of ideas. He was also very restless. It was obvious that he was suffering from a bipolar affective disorder and he began treatment with lithium carbonate. He responded well.

K has continued to take lithium carbonate, a prophylactic mood stabiliser, for over five years. Both he and his wife are fully aware of the nature of his illness and of the need for him to take lithium on a long-term basis.

Disorders of volition

Loss of self control

Aggression, whether oral or physical, is not unusual in people with mental disorders. There may be more than one cause. It can generate anxiety and hostility and, if not understood, carers may over-react.

Aggression may result from organic, psychological or psychiatric causes or a combination of these. Organic factors include cerebral dysrhythmia of any aetiology, clouding of consciousness due to such causes as alcohol or drugs, both prescribed or illicit, or to generalised bodily illness such as anaemia or an infective illness.

Aggression can occur when there is poor self-control such as in mental impairment or personality disorders. It may occur in hypomania or mania when it is often associated with frustration and irritability. It can occur in schizophrenia due to delusional ideation. Aggressive behaviour can also be a response to a frightening or frustrating experience and can almost always be traced to disturbed interpersonal relationships, It is commonplace in childhood (temper tantrums) and, not surprisingly, in immature deaf people, especially those who have poor language skills and/or cerebral dysfunction.

Deaf people frequently experience frustration when attempting to communicate with hearing people. Moreover, their inability to express dissatisfaction or anger in the normal way, or quickly enough, by emotionally toned vocalisation, may lead to the physical display of such feelings (Denmark 1966). This 'acting out', which at times may be explosive in nature, may be mistakenly attributed to mental disorder. This behaviour most commonly occurs in immature preverbal deaf people but may occur whatever the type of deafness.

> MA, a 20-year-old preverbally profoundly deaf young man, was admitted as an emergency to the psychiatric department of a general hospital one evening under an assessment order of the Mental Health Act 1959 after assaulting his father. The police had been called to his home, whereupon he became so disturbed that he had been handcuffed to get him into an ambulance. The admitting doctor had written in his case notes 'He is tense and anxious. Unable to get a history as he is deaf and dumb.'

> The following morning, M was seen by the author. He was without speech and had poor verbal language but communicated reasonably well using sign language and, within the limits of his verbal language, by fingerspelling. Initially, he was apprehensive, but was relieved when he found that the author could communicate with him. He explained

that he had become upset following a difference of opinion with a workmate who had previously befriended him. He was afraid that, as a consequence, he might lose his only friend at work. On the way home from work he felt depressed and went into a public house for a couple of pints of beer. When he arrived home his parents noticed there was something wrong with him. He tried to explain but they could not use sign language and did not understand him. He became frustrated and angry and left the room, slamming the door. His father had followed him and had taken hold of him from behind. He became very angry and struck his father. He was sorry for what had happened.

Later that day M's parents were interviewed. They confirmed the history given by their son. They related that he had been born deaf and had been educated at a school for deaf children. The school had adopted a purely oral approach to communication. They had been told that their son would learn to speak and that under no circumstances should they use sign language or fingerspelling. If tempted to use gesture, they had been told that they should sit on their hands! Initially, they had accepted this advice but later regretted accepting it. They confirmed the history given by their son and, after a discussion on methods of communication, both parents vowed that the would learn both fingerspelling and sign language. M was immediately discharged.

❄ ❄ ❄ ❄ ❄ ❄

LD, aged 23 years, was remanded for psychiatric reports to a Remand Centre in the south of England, having been charged with assault. He had been born profoundly deaf and with a hemiparesis and had suffered from epilepsy from birth. He was educated at two schools for deaf children, both of which adopted a purely oral approach to communication. However, he never learned to speak and had limited English language.

L had met a young partially hearing woman at a deaf club who had agreed to go out with him. They arranged that he would call for her at her home. When he called at the house her mother answered the door. There were communication problems but it became apparent that the girl's mother did not want him to see her daughter. She gestured that she wanted him to leave. He did not, so she pushed him. He became angry and retaliated in like fashion. She called the police and he was arrested. The medical officer of the Remand Centre had written:

He grunts in a manneristic way. The diagnosis is difficult to assess but by his general demeanor he could be schizophrenic or mentally defective or anything. He has a look of a schizophrenic dullard.

L communicated by sign language and, within the limits of his verbal language, by fingerspelling. He gave a reasonable account. There was no evidence of mental illness nor did he appear to be intellectually impaired. Understandably, he felt aggrieved at having been sent to 'prison'. (He had no understanding of the word 'remand' and his status had not been explained to him.) A report was sent to the medical officer who enclosed it with his own report to the court. When L appeared in court he was given a conditional discharge.

L was followed up at an out-patient clinic where he was assessed psychometrically. He was of average intelligence.

The following case history illustrates the problems of a man who became deaf postlingually and the difficulties in examining him.

HT, a 64-year-old profoundly deaf man, was seen in consultation in the psychiatric department of a general hospital at the request of a consultant psychiatrist who had seen him on a domiciliary visit. He had assaulted his wife. The psychiatrist had great difficulty in communicating with him and decided to admit him for assessment. He had become disturbed on admission and had been given intramuscular psychotropic medication to calm him.

After much enquiry including study of H's general practitioner's case file and an interview with the patient's wife, the author obtained the following history. He had become profoundly deaf in both ears in his early thirties but the cause was not known. He was married to a woman who did not have any real understanding of his problems. He was a poor lipreader and they had great difficulty in communicating with each other.

Not long after becoming deaf, H had struck his wife during an argument and he was admitted to a mental hospital. He was thought to have a 'paranoid illness'. He remained in hospital for some few weeks and, as he had shown no disturbed behaviour, had been discharged home. A few years later they moved to another town.

H's current admission had been precipitated by another marital dispute. His wife had complained to the general practitioner that he had hit her. The doctor had studied his case file, noted a previous admission and requested the domiciliary visit which led to the admission.

H was profoundly deaf. There were marked rhythmical movements of all limbs and he appeared to have generalised rigidity. He had difficulty in speaking partly, it seemed, because his speech had deteriorated, but probably also because of the medication. There were serious receptive difficulties also, for he was a poor lipreader and his spectacles had been left at home.

H's examination had to be undertaken using paper and pencil and took over four hours. He gave an account of the difficulties he encountered because of his deafness and of the marital friction. However, he did not appear to have any paranoid ideas. It also transpired that the patient had been admitted informally and that his rights had not been explained to him. Had they been, he would not have agreed to admission, he said.

The involuntary movements appeared to be due to the medication and, at the author's suggestion, this was discontinued apart from a drug to ameliorate the side effects. After further discussion, H agreed to remain in hospital for a few days to make sure the side effects would disappear.

H was seen again three weeks after his discharge. There had been no further problems. He and his wife agreed to see a social worker with deaf people for counselling and support.

Problems of behaviour and adjustment

Research has shown that many young deaf people with hearing parents present problems of behaviour and adjustment within the home, at school, at work or in the community. These problems often lead to referral to social workers or mental health agencies, or to appearance in the courts.

Workers have attributed such traits as egocentricity, lack of foresight, inability to empathise and impulsive and aggressive behaviour to such young deaf people (Basilier 1964). Workers who are not *au fait* with the psycho-social aspects of deafness may construe that these traits are symptomatic of personality disorders *per se*, assuming that the prognosis, as with hearing people, may be poor.

Some of the features described may, in some instances, result from genetic and/or organic factors such as minimal brain dysfunction. (The latter may be due to the same agent responsible for the deafness, see Appendix One.) However, research has also shown that deaf children who have deaf parents and have been brought up using sign language and are integrated members of the family are not likely to present such problems and are better adjusted both emotionally and socially. It follows, therefore, that nurture rather than nature is the cause. In other words, the immature personalities of many preverbally deaf children are the result of poor early parent–child relationships and the child's lack of an effective means of communication in the early formative years. Sadly, the problems are often compounded by inappropriate educational methods and unrealistic parental expectations resulting from misguided advice from professionals, who perceive a deaf child's identity with deaf culture and the deaf community as a sign of failure. Indeed, many parents have felt a sense of loss when their children have adopted a deaf identity.

Experience has shown that if young deaf people with behaviour and adjustment problems can be involved in appropriate therapeutic programmes in a deaf milieu, the prognosis may be good. However, the most important need is the development of preventive mental health programmes aimed at enabling deaf children to become fully integrated members of their own families. This is only possible if parents of very young deaf children are given counselling and appropriate guidance in respect of the need for sign language in the early years, and recognition that their child's mental health may be adversely affected if denied access to deaf culture and the deaf community.

Basilier (1964), a Norwegian psychiatrist, coined the term 'Surdophrenia' to describe the behaviour and adjustment problems commonly seen in young deaf people. However, the term has rightly fallen into disrepute for a number of reasons. It may be mistakenly associated with schizophrenia or it may give the mistaken impression that all young deaf people have these characteristics. It also suggests that such problems are the result of deafness itself, whereas in reality they are often due to lack of effective help in the formative years.

The need for many deaf children to use sign language is continually being underlined in a department where the main medium of communication is sign language. Comments or questions of relatives such as 'Can you tell my son that I love him?' or 'How do I tell her that I will visit her again next week?' are common. Two student teachers of deaf children had been told by their teacher not to read the author's article entitled 'The Education of Deaf Children'(Denmark 1973). They were emotionally upset on visiting the department because, in two years' training, they had never met a profoundly deaf child or adult.

Behaviour problems are not confined to preverbally profoundly deaf young people. They can occur when children have unrecognised partial deafness. Difficulties in understanding may lead to frustration and disturbed behaviour both at home and in school. It is important, therefore, that all children are screened for hearing impairments at the beginning of school life and that when they do not make normal progress they undergo audiometric testing.

Withdrawal

Post-lingual deafness can lead to withdrawal from social contact. However, most deafened people come to terms with their disability so that, when withdrawal is a predominant feature, other causes should be considered. Withdrawal is not usually associated with preverbal deafness and when it occurs in such a setting it invariably indicates other pathology. (It can be a feature of schizophrenia and also occurs in depressive and in some organic states.)

SB, a preverbally profoundly deaf young woman, was referred by a physician in audiological medicine. He wrote:

> This young deaf woman has been attending here with her parents for some years. She began to isolate herself in her late 'teens and has progressively become more and more withdrawn. We now think she may have other psychological problems in addition to those related to her deafness and would welcome your advice.

According to her mother, S was born profoundly deaf, but the cause was unknown. She had been a pupil at a residential school for deaf children as a weekly boarder and was said to have been an average scholar. She never learned to speak intelligibly and the rest of the family had great difficulty in communicating with her. They had been advised against using sign language or fingerspelling and she communicated with the rest of the family by gesture and writing.

After leaving school, S worked as a punch-card operator and was a happy young woman. She enjoyed needlework and horseriding with a group of hearing children. She had no close friends but occasionally visited the nearest deaf club.

When she was 18 years old she began to isolate herself, spent long periods alone in her bedroom and neglected her appearance. Eventually she lost her job because of poor attendance.

S appeared to be apathetic and withdrawn. She made no spontaneous attempts to communicate but it was possible to demonstrate that she had facility in both sign language and fingerspelling. However, she gave a poor account. She had no complaints or worries. She was not anxious or depressed. To most questions she replied, using sign language, 'I don't know'. She was thought to be suffering from simple schizophrenia.

S was admitted to hospital for observation and treatment. On the day of admission, her mother brought a photograph of her taken shortly after she left school. She presented an entirely different picture from that of her present state. She was sitting on a horse, smiling and obviously happy and alert. She was fully investigated physically but no abnormality was found. Enquiries revealed that her aunt suffered from schizophrenia. In spite of intensive individual and group therapy and trials on different psychotropic medication, however, she remained self-absorbed and lacking in motivation and was eventually was discharged home. There is little doubt that the diagnosis was correct.

Disorders of thinking

Disorders of thinking include disorders of form and disorders of content.

Disorders of form

Some of the signs of mental illness, such as the pressure of thought of mania and the retardation of thought of psychotic depression, can be detected in preverbally profoundly deaf patients, provided psychiatrists have the requisite skills and experience.

Schizophrenic thought disorder can present in many ways. It may be subjective or objective. Some patients complain of difficulty in thinking, while in others the phenomenon is rather objective. There may be difficulty in conceptual thinking, or it may be manifest by a certain vagueness. Preverbally deaf people with limited sign language skills tend to think in concrete terms and this may be difficult to differentiate from the concrete thinking seen in schizophrenia.

It is important not to conclude that the poor account given by a preverbally deaf patient is a consequence of their limited language. Deterioration in a person's ability to communicate may be due to a number of causes, including the poverty of ideation or disordered thinking of a schizophrenic illness, the retardation of thought of a depressive illness, or even an organic reaction. An independent history is often helpful in such circumstances and should always be sought.

Mrs J was referred by her general practitioner at the suggestion of a social worker with deaf people. The social worker explained that he, himself, had only recently become profoundly deaf in both ears, that he had only been fairly recently been appointed, that he had not had any social work training and could not communicate by sign language! Nevertheless, from the information he had received from her two cousins, he felt that his client needed psychiatric assessment. The background history was obtained from the social worker and two cousins. Unfortunately, neither of the cousins, nor any other members of the family, had any facility in sign language.

Mrs J had been born profoundly deaf. There was no family history of deafness but a paternal aunt had been treated in a mental hospital.

Mrs J had attended a school for deaf children which adopted a purely oral approach to communication. She had never learned to speak and her verbal language was poor.

Mrs J had married a partially hearing man. However, there was marital discord from the start and they had separated and eventually divorced. Mrs J returned to her parents' home, but her mother and then her father died. She had some deaf friends but she rarely saw them and did not attend the local deaf club.

Mrs J had been prone to 'tantrums' all her life but in the two years before her mother died she had frequently attacked her parents. They could not understand why she did so. More recently she had begun to neglect herself and on one or two occasions had hit strangers in the street with an umbrella. On another occasion she threatened one of her cousins with a knife.

Mrs J was a small, obese, pale woman. Her face was a little puffy and suggestive of hypothyroidism. She was without speech and had poor verbal language. She had some facility in sign language but her verbal language appeared to be poor and she gave a very poor account. It was difficult to understand much of what she was trying to convey. The clinical picture was that of a paranoid state and the differential diagnosis was thought to rest between an organic reaction associated with myxoedema and paranoid schizophrenia.

Mrs J was unwilling to enter hospital and so it was agreed that arrangements would be made to investigate her thyroid function on an out-patient basis. However, she would not cooperate and so was admitted formally to hospital under the Mental Health Act.

Mrs J did not settle. She did not mix with the other patients and was frequently hostile in manner. She was investigated and found to be myxoedematous. However, in spite of treatment for this, her mental condition remained unchanged. After attempts to involve her in a variety of programmes including individual, group and occupational, therapy there was no change in her condition. She was thought to be suffering from a paranoid psychosis and, after consultation with her relatives, she was prescribed psychotropic medication.

With medication, not only did Mrs.J's behaviour quickly change in that she became pleasant and co-operative, but her ability to communicate improved rapidly also. She recalled having thought that people were trying to harm her and soon gained good insight. She was discharged with arrangements to continue medication from her own doctor and to be reviewed as an out-patient. She remains well and has become an active member of her local deaf club.

ECHOLALIA

Speech is possible without language. Parrots can speak. Echolalia is the meaningless imitation of the speech of others. It often signifies a desire to communicate but an inability so to do. It sometimes occurs in hearing people with chronic schizophrenia or with severe mental impairment.

ECHOPRAXIA

Echopraxia is the meaningless imitation of actions of others. When attempts are made to communicate with a deaf person who exhibits echopraxia, the subject will respond by copying the fingerspelling, sign language or gesture of the person who is attempting to communicate with him or her.

When echopraxia occurs in deaf subjects, it can be the result of mental impairment, or a long-standing psychosis. It can also indicate a desire to communicate but an inability to do so, for whatever reason.

Disorders of content

When patients have communication problems it may be difficult to determine whether comments are delusional or not. It is important not to conclude that comments that appear to be bizarre are delusional until all possible explanations have been considered. Patients may simply be recounting their conversations with other deaf people, or commenting on events seen on television.

NEOLOGISMS

Neologisms are newly coined words. They are sometimes occur in schizophrenia. They should not be confused with the spelling mistakes made by
deaf people with limited verbal language, but the possibility should be
considered.

PARANOID IDEAS, PARANOID PSYCHOSES AND DEAFNESS

A relationship between deafness and paranoia has been postulated for a long
time (Levine 1960, Slater and Roth 1972). One study showed that there was
an excess of elderly patients with paranoid psychosis who had been partially
deaf from early or middle age (Cooper, Garside and Kay 1976). However,
there is no evidence to support the view that deafness gives rise to paranoid
reactions or that paranoid psychoses are any more prevalent among people
who have been deaf from early life (Thomas 1981).

Abnormal perceptual experiences

Deaf people with limited language may have difficulty in describing abnormal experiences. Some of these experiences, such as ideas of reference, may
be not too difficult to express but others, such as pressure of thought,
thought blocking or passivity phenomena may be difficult to describe.

Hallucinations

Hallucinations are a common symptom of schizophrenia. The commonest
hallucinations in normally hearing people are auditory and usually take the
form of voices being heard. Auditory hallucinations take the same form in
postlingually deaf and partially deaf schizophrenics. (In the former this is
apparently because they have auditory memories.) However, they would not
be expected to occur in preverbally profoundly deaf schizophrenics. Research confirms that they do not occur, but that visual and haptic hallucinations are common. The former often take the form of ghosts or of people
communicating with the subject by sign language and/or fingerspelling.

> One morning when the author arrived at the hospital he was greeted
> by some half a dozen young female patients who were eager to inform
> him that they had all seen a ghost during the preceding night. As most
> of the patients were not psychotic, this appeared to be a surprising
> phenomenon. Further enquiry, however, revealed that a bright young
> non-psychotic patient, having been informed by another that she had
> seen ghosts, decided to play a prank on some others by awakening

them during the night with a bed sheet draped over her head and upper body!

When examining deaf patients with limited sign language it is often difficult to determine the exact nature of their subjective experiences especially as leading questions may have to be asked. Moreover, some patients use the sign 'talk' to describe experiences which are clearly not auditory or visual. It appears that they are describing experiences that are analogous to auditory hallucinations (Critchley, Denmark, Warren and Wilson 1981).

BK was 35 years old when he was referred by a consultant psychiatrist at the suggestion of a social worker with deaf people. The presenting problem was one of alcoholism.

B had been born profoundly deaf. He was educated in a residential school for deaf children which adopted an oral/only approach. However, he never learned to speak and when he left school he had only limited verbal language and poor scholastic achievements. After leaving school he worked first in a bakery and then helped delivering milk. Finally, he obtained a job as a part time postman.

B's family had great difficulty in communicating with him and he had few friends. He was said to be irritable at times, especially under the influence of alcohol. He drank to excess and was often drunk.

Two years before his referral, B had been admitted to a local mental hospital and was thought to be suffering from schizophrenia.

B communicated by sign language with some fingerspelling. He 'said', using sign language, that he had seen lots of doctors and was surprised to meet someone who could use sign language. He complained that everywhere he walked he was followed and that when he stopped those following him stopped also. He did not know who they were or why they followed him. He complained that someone or somebody was trying to take something out of his head. He thought the people involved were from London where a deaf girl named Molly who had been a schoolmate was living. He thought he had been ill for about two years. He had difficulty in communicating with people. Sometimes he felt 'mixed up'. He liked to drink. It made him feel better. Acquaintances bought him drinks. He had seen Christ. There was no doubt that he was suffering from a paranoid psychosis. He was admitted informally for treatment.

One day, B reported that his friend Molly had been talking to him from London. He explained that he often saw her. She appeared above him.

He could see the upper part of her body. She signed to him. He could see her at that moment. B had been asking to leave hospital but had been persuaded to remain for treatment. The topic arose again. He was asked, in a somewhat teasing manner, what Molly would think. He raised his eyes as though looking into the distance and signed, 'Doctor Denmark wants me to stay in hospital. What do you think?' There was a pause. He then raised his eyebrows and nodded. 'What did she say?' he was asked. 'She thinks I should stay!' he replied.

Tinnitus

Tinnitus is the perception of sound in the absence of an acoustic stimulus and which is due to a disorder of the hearing mechanism. It is most commonly associated with post-lingual deafness but can occur in all types. It can take various forms, including ringing, whistling or buzzing.

Tinnitus can sometimes be difficult to differentiate from hallucinations as the latter may be elementary and not always perceived as voices talking.

DC, a 34-year-old deaf man, had been referred to a psychiatrist by his general practitioner. He had been 'increasingly complaining that people had been critical and passing adverse remarks about him'. The psychiatrist could not communicate directly with the patient but had to rely upon his brother who could communicate with him by sign language. The psychiatrist found it difficult to decide whether D 'was becoming psychotic' or whether his symptoms were 'secondary to his deafness'.

D was accompanied to an out-patient clinic by his brother and a social worker with deaf people. The latter had previously sent a very comprehensive social history which suggested that he suffered from tinnitus and had also become anxious and had nightmares when he was left alone at home while his mother and grandmother with whom he lived went on holiday.

D had been a full term baby and the delivery was normal. However, he never talked and, at the age of four years, he was found to be deaf. He was educated in a residential school for deaf children but never learned to speak. He was prescribed hearing aids but never wore them after leaving school. His parents were divorced. It was reported that he could communicate reasonably well with his mother by lipreading and some sign language, but that his grandmother had to write if she wanted to communicate with him. He had been knocked down by a motor vehicle some five years previously and had been unconscious for five hours.

The history obtained from his brother and his social worker was that D had complained of head noises for about four years. They were worse at night and caused insomnia, for which his general practitioner had prescribed hypnotics. Some 18 months before he was seen he had become afraid of being alone and afraid to leave home. He had complained that people were looking at him, laughing at him and photographing him. He thought that someone in a motor car had tried to knock him down and that his mother had put something in his tea.

D presented as a preverbally profoundly deaf man of good intelligence. He communicated well by sign language and, within the limits of his verbal language, by fingerspelling. He gave a good account.

D explained that he had experienced head noises for about five years. They were 'like banging, people's voices, like scratching, a biting noise', going round his head. Three years previously, while reading a newspaper, he had seen a white flash. He 'dreamed' of God's face, of Jesus. He sometimes saw God's face and that of Jesus when he was awake. He had seen hundreds of God's faces looking at the earth. He was afraid to go out. People wanted to masturbate him. They wanted his sperm. People on the television wanted him to masturbate. They had gestured at him sexually. His penis had become sore. Physical examination revealed no abnormality.

D was undoubtedly suffering from a paranoid psychosis presenting with delusions of a religious and paranoid nature and with auditory and visual hallucinations. His name was put on the waiting list for admission. In the meantime, it was suggested that he was treated with Trifluperazine, an antipsychotic drug. However, when a bed was available six months later, he had improved greatly and admission was not necessary. Apart from his head noises he was not only free of all his other symptoms but had no worries. His brother, moreover, felt that he was better than he had been for many years.

D's mental state remained improved, but he continued to complain of throbbing in his left ear. It interfered with his sleep if he slept on his left side but not his right. He was referred to a physician in audiological medicine and fully investigated but no physical abnormality was detected.

D was followed up as an out-patient for six years. There continued to be no evidence of psychotic symptoms, but he continued to complain of head noises. There seemed little doubt that he suffered from both paranoid schizophrenia with auditory hallucinations and with tinnitus.

Disorders of intellect

Disorders of intellect include mental impairment (amentia) and intellectual deterioration (dementia).

Mental impairment

Deaf people may be mistakenly thought to be mentally impaired for a number of reasons. Mental impairment is the commonest cause of failure to develop speech and it is probably for this reason that the word 'dumb' is used colloquially with this meaning. There is, therefore, the danger that anyone without speech may be so regarded.

In a clinical situation, if attempts are made to examine a preverbally profoundly deaf person with poor verbal language using the written word, even simple questions may not be understood or they may be misunderstood. Even if they are understood, answers may be given using poor verbal language. Such responses may be mistakenly thought to be further evidence of low intelligence.

Further difficulties may arise when preverbally deaf patients undergo psychometric testing. If the psychologist cannot communicate effectively with them he will be unable to put them at ease, to explain the nature of the situation or properly give instructions. The results of testing may therefore be affected. Moreover, if the psychologist is unaware of the psycholinguistic problems, inappropriate tests may be used. If verbally loaded tests are used, many preverbally profoundly deaf patients will score badly and the consequences may be disastrous.

> EF was 54 years old when he was seen in a survey of deaf patients in a hospital for the mentally impaired. He had been a pupil in a school for the deaf from the age of 4 until 14 years. His mother was a single parent and she said that she could not manage him, so he was admitted to a Poor Law Institution. He had been admitted to hospital at the age of 16 years under the Mental Deficiency Acts 1913–1938. A statement made by a doctor at that time was as follows:
>
> > *His general appearance and attitude are childish, as compared with others of his age. He is fidgety and abrupt in his manner. This boy being*

dumb, my estimate of his intelligence is based upon my observation of his conduct during the past two years (Oct 1st 1925–Oct 1st 1927). He is childish in manner and behaviour, and is at times very emotional without adequate reasons. He does not take a normal interest in things and is unable to concentrate his attention on anything for long at once.

The following day the certifying doctor had written:

Is apparently completely deaf and dumb. Cannot read ordinary printed matter. He can write his name but little else. Diagnosis. Feeble-minded Deaf Mute.

The admitting doctor had written:

He is feeble-minded; he is a deaf mute who appears to appreciate no sounds at all and who is completely incapable of articulate speech. He can comprehend only the very simplest printed or type-written questions or requests. Quite fails to do the reading comprehension test year 7(Burt). Throughout examination he was excitable and nervous. Attention and concentration not good.

E had been in hospital for 38 years. He presented as an anxious but pleasant man. He was profoundly deaf and without speech but could communicate, albeit at a limited level, by sign language and, within the limits of his verbal language, by fingerspelling. (His verbal language was limited.) He was well orientated and gave a reasonable account of his life history. He related that his father had died when he was a young child, that he had attended a school which did not allow the use of sign language or fingerspelling. Children were punished by caning if found so doing. Neither his mother nor his older brother could communicate with him. His mother had died some years previously. He complained that he was unhappy in hospital and wished to live with other deaf people with whom he could communicate by sign language.

According to members of the nursing staff E presented no problems apart from the fact that at times he complained of abdominal pains. These were thought to be hypochondriacal as he would not complain for months at a time. He worked in the tailor's shop and had parole both in the grounds of the hospital and to go into the local village.

He readily accepted the offer of transfer to a hospital where the author worked and where there were other deaf patients and this was duly arranged.

E was delighted to be amongst other patients and staff with whom he could communicate easily. On psychometric testing he achieved a performance intelligence quotient of 104.

Shortly after admission E again complained of abdominal pain. Palpation of the abdomen revealed tenderness in the epigastrium and rectal examination showed that he had melaena. X-rays confirmed the presence of an active duodenal ulcer. He underwent surgery and made a good recovery. He was eventually discharged to a hostel for deaf people. He was found employment in a motorcar showroom where he washed and polished cars, spending 13 years there until he retired at the age of 74.

❧ ❧ ❧ ❧ ❧ ❧

FJ, a 22-year-old Scotswoman, was referred by a consultant psychiatrist for 'assessment and treatment'. She had been admitted to a hospital for the mentally impaired some 12 months previously. It was said that nobody could communicate with her effectively there. The following history was obtained. She was one of five children, one of them having Down's syndrome. F became profoundly deaf in early childhood as the result of tuberculous meningitis and at the age of six years developed tuberculosis of the left hip joint. She had been educated at a residential school for deaf children. Her mother died when she was 11 years old and her father rejected her.

F left school at the age of 16 years and entered a hostel for the physically handicapped. At the age of 21 years she was admitted to hospital for amputation of her left lower leg and afterwards became very depressed. It seemed that she had hoped that the surgery would make her like other girls and that she would be able to walk, run and dance. She was discharged back to the hostel where she was described as 'moody and difficult'. She often returned late and 'the worse for drink'. She said that she disliked the hostel and wanted a flat of her own. However, her social worker considered that 'her intelligence and physical disability would prevent her from living independently and working in open industry'.

F was referred to a psychiatrist who described her as 'dull and backward' and arranged for her admission to a hospital for the mentally impaired. She was prescribed antidepressant medication and referred to the author.

It was decided to admit the patient for a period of assessment and she was eventually transferred. She was found to be a pleasant, bright-eyed, profoundly deaf young woman. She had a severe degree of hearing impairment. Although she had some hearing with amplification, she was unable to understand speech. She had poor verbal language. However, she gave a good account using sign language. She did not appear to be unintelligent.

F was pleased to be admitted to the Department. She settled immediately and no depression was evident. The medication was withdrawn with no change in her mood. It became apparent that she had expected a better and immediate result from the surgery and was unaware that she would require a period of rehabilitation before she could walk on her artificial leg properly. Psychometric assessment showed that she was of average intelligence, for she achieved a Performance Scale Intelligence Quotient of 104 on the Wechsler Adult Intelligence Scale.

F proved to be a somewhat immature young woman. On a number of occasions she reacted to minimal stress with aggressive behaviour. She was involved in a number of programmes including individual and group therapy, education and occupational therapy and her behaviour gradually improved. She was discharged to a hostel for deaf people and soon found employment in a factory. After approximately a year she found her own apartment had, within this period, integrated well into the local deaf community.

Partial deafness in childhood may go unrecognised and any developmental delay may be mistakenly attributed to mental impairment.

NM was eight years, eight months old when his mother sought an appointment to discuss his education. She was concerned because her son had been transferred from a regular school to a school for children with learning difficulties. She related that she had thought her son had a hearing problem when he was about four years old and had sought the advice of her general practitioner.

He had performed only a superficial examination and told her that there was nothing wrong with her child and that she was worrying unnecessarily.

N developed speech and language, albeit a little slowly, and began primary school at four years ten months. However, his progress was poor and at the age of seven years he was transferred to a school for slow learning children. Shortly after his transfer he was thought by the school doctor to have a hearing impairment and this was confirmed by audiometry. Otological examination had revealed bilateral serous otitis media. Grommets were inserted into both tympanic membranes and his hearing improved considerably.

N was a bright little boy. His speech was fair but his command of language was poor. On psychometric testing he achieved a full scale intelligence quotient of 102. A report was sent to his local Education Officer and he was transferred to a school for normal children.

When mental impairment occurs in a setting of preverbal deafness it may be difficult to determine the degrees of either. Moreover, either the deafness or the mental impairment may be overlooked. If the person is obviously deaf, poor functioning due to coexistent mental impairment may be overlooked and the poor functioning attributed to this alone.

Conversely, when individuals are obviously mentally impaired, the fact that they have a hearing impairment may not be recognised.

Deaf people with significant degrees of mental impairment often do not receive appropriate help and their potential is often underestimated. Exposure to sign language systems can bring about remarkable changes in their social functioning, their life-style and their happiness.

Dementia

Dementia is deterioration of intellect. It is common in late age, less common in middle age (presenile dementia) and, rarely, can occur in adolescence and even in childhood.

Dementia is usually of insidious onset and when deaf people have difficulty in functioning, workers need to be aware that such a disorder may exist.

HD, an 80-year-old profoundly deaf woman without speech, was seen at a Home for deaf women where she had been admitted some weeks previously, following the death of her husband. She had been unable to manage on her own after his death and had failed to settle in the Home. It was thought that she might be suffering from a depressive reaction.

H had reasonable verbal language and had good skills in both fingerspelling and sign language. She appeared to be in good general health and smiled readily. However, she was disorientated in time and place and had marked impairment of memory. Although she was able to give a reasonable account of her distant past she had no idea of the day, date, month or year or her whereabouts. She knew her date of birth but thought she was 'about 40' years old. No physical abnormality was found.

H was admitted to hospital for a short period to exclude any treatable condition. Investigations all proved negative apart from a brain scan which showed gross generalised cortical atrophy. H was suffering from Alzheimer's disease.

PITFALLS IN THE PSYCHIATRIC AND PSYCHOLOGICAL ASSESSMENT OF DEAF PEOPLE

It follows from the study of the ways in which deafness may affect the presentation of mental disorder that there are many pitfalls in the psychiatric and psychological assessment of deaf people. These pitfalls can be summarised as follows:

Mental illness may not be recognised

Communication problems may mask mental illness

The communication problems of some deaf people may mask the presence of mental illness, sometimes for many years. Unfortunately, many social workers with deaf people are not trained in mental health issues and may not recognise the presence of mental illness in their clients.

EL, a 54-year-old prelingually profoundly deaf man, was referred by his general practitioner at the suggestion of a social worker with deaf people. The social worker was a deafened man with good sign language skills, but he had not received any formal training in social work or in mental health issues. In his referral, letter he had written.

> *I would be grateful if you would see this client of mine. For over a year he has had numerous complaints. He has had all his teeth removed, his sinuses washed out and his gall bladder and appendix removed, all without any change. He is quite depressed.*

E was profoundly deaf and without speech but communicated well by sign language and by fingerspelling. He was overtly depressed and had numerous somatic complaints. His appetite was poor and he had lost nearly a stone in weight. His depression was worse in the morning and he had terminal insomnia. He had lost interest and thought he had cancer and was going to die. Physical examination revealed no abnormality.

There seemed little doubt that E was suffering from an severe depressive illness presenting with hypochondriasis. He was admitted informally and responded quickly to treatment with antidepressant medication. He was discharged home, symptom-free, and having put on nearly half a stone in weight after six weeks.

Symptoms of mental disorder may be mistakenly attributed to deafness

Depression and withdrawal from social contact are sometimes associated with postlingual deafness. However, it should not be presumed that this is necessarily the case and when they occur in a setting of preverbal deafness other causes must be considered.

It is also important to understand that when deaf people have communication difficulties, they may be due to such causes as mental impairment, mental illness, or other less common causes such as specific language disorders.

Mental illness may be mistakenly diagnosed

Communication problems may mistakenly be attributed to mental illness

When deaf people are unable to communicate easily with hearing people frustration may result. In such circumstances, the physical display of emotion may not be understood and mistakenly attributed to mental illness.

Difficulties in conceptualising may be mistaken for mental illness

Some preverbally deaf people have limited ability to communicate both in sign language and in verbal language. This may be due to the presence of disabilities or due to lack of exposure to sign language in childhood. The resulting difficulties in conceptualisation may be mistakenly thought to be due to schizophrenia.

Symptoms due to physical disease may be mistakenly attributed to mental illness

Physical illness can present with symptoms of mental disorder and unless mental health workers can communicate effectively with deaf people, mistakes in diagnosis may be made.

LA, a 48-year-old prelingually profoundly deaf, man was seen as an out patient. He was accompanied by his social worker, a specialist worker with deaf people, who had been involved with him for nearly two years. She gave the following account:

L was a refuse collector. He was married to a preverbally profoundly deaf woman. There had apparently been no problems until she, the social worker, had been approached by the patient because he had abdominal pain and requested that she should accompany him to his general practitioner in order to interpret for him. The doctor had listened to the account given by the patient through his social worker and conducted a physical examination. He had arranged a barium meal X-Ray but this revealed no abnormality, and so the patient was informed.

L had continued to experience symptoms but also began to wake during the night. He began to lose weight and eventually came off work. His failure to go to work led to marital friction and after some months his wife left him.

L continued to complain of abdominal pains and became overtly depressed. He had felt that life was not worth living. His social worker had spent a placement on the Department at Whittingham Hospital and had learned that somatic complaints may be hypochondriacal and due to depressive illness. She sought an appointment but when informed that the waiting time for an out-patient appointment was over 12 months she asked the general practitioner to refer the patient to a local psychiatrist.

L was subsequently seen locally as an out-patient by a psychiatrist with the social worker as an interpreter and at the end of the interview he asked the social worker what she thought was wrong. She said that he appeared to be depressed, had lost weight, awoke in the night and appeared to be hypochondriacal. She thought, she said that he had a depressive illness and the psychiatrist accepted her opinion.

The psychiatrist at first treated L with antidepressant medication, but to no avail, and decided to give him a course of electro-convulsive therapy. Again there was no change in his condition.

L was eventually seen as an out-patient by the author. He was an intelligent man who gave a good account using sign language. He appeared to be underweight and anxious. He began by explaining that he was convinced that there was something physically wrong and that it was a mistake to believe that there was something wrong with his mind. He accepted that he was depressed but insisted that his depression was because he continued to have pain, because his wife had left him and because doctors thought he was mentally ill.

L gave a history consistent with a gastric ulcer. He had epigastric pain which was usually made worse by eating. His stools were invariably dark in colour. He felt tired and could not do his job, which was a heavy one. Often he could not sleep. Physical examination revealed epigastric tenderness and rectal examination showed melaena.

L was relieved when told that he probably had a gastric ulcer but could not understand how this had not been found previously. He was re-X-Rayed and found to have a large gastric ulcer. He underwent surgery with complete relief of his symptoms.

☙ ☙ ☙ ☙ ☙ ☙

CW, a 24-year-old deaf woman, was admitted having been referred as a matter of urgency by a consultant psychiatrist in a hospital some 150 miles from Whittingham Hospital. She had been admitted to her local hospital with a fractured jaw but had been unco-operative and disturbed. The local social worker with deaf people had been unable to communicate with her and she had been incontinent of urine and occasionally of faeces also.

The history given by the referring doctor was as follows: She was the eldest of three children. She was born deaf but there was no family history and no obvious cause was found.

C had attended a residential school for deaf children from the age of four years until she was 16. She apparently had a moderate degree of deafness and had intelligible speech. She was said to be semi-literate. She was reported to have communicated by speech and lipreading but 'also used sign language'. Her scholastic achievements were poor.

C had a hearing boyfriend. She became pregnant and they married. Subsequently, she gave birth to a baby boy. Grave doubts were expressed about her ability to care for the child and she was provided with a volunteer helper and a home help in addition to support from a health visitor and a social worker. However, she became uncommunicative and withdrawn and her personal habits deteriorated. She would wipe her nose on the back of her hand and then lick it. She ate the contents of sandwiches with her fingers and failed to wash herself or change her clothing. Her husband became angry with her and hit her. He fractured her jaw.

Following treatment for her fracture, C had been transferred to the psychiatric department. She was fully investigated physically, including a brain scan, but no abnormality had been found. She was thought to be mentally impaired and suffering from a puerperal psychosis.

C was transferred to Whittingham Hospital and admitted to the deaf unit as an informal patient. She had to helped from the ambulance. She was withdrawn and uncommunicative. On one occasion when asked her name she replied '77712'. She was doubly incontinent and needed total care.

At first C was thought to have a severe puerperal psychosis but in spite of treatment her condition failed to improve. Although her family lived at some distance from the hospital, it was felt that the history which had been obtained previously should be confirmed. It then transpired that she had seemed 'a little odd' even before she had become pregnant and had began to withdraw at quite an early stage. A repeated physical examination then showed signs indicative of intracranial pathology and she was referred for a neurological opinion. Further investigation then showed evidence of a diffuse abnormality mainly affecting the frontal lobes.

C's condition gradually deteriorated and she died. A post mortem revealed that she had been suffering from Schilder's disease.

Mental impairment may be mistakenly diagnosed

Mental impairment is the commonest cause of failure to talk and people without speech may mistakenly thought to be mentally impaired.

MT was referred by the Superintendent of a Society for the Deaf with a long history of behaviour and adjustment problems. He had no general practitioner.

MT was of low birth weight, weighing only four pounds. His speech was delayed in onset and he was diagnosed as partially deaf at the age of 20 months. He was educated at two residential schools for deaf children where he was regarded as maladjusted. He was rejected by his parents and spent the holidays of his last years at school in care. After leaving school he was employed in a number of jobs for short periods only, being dismissed for poor time-keeping, poor performance and abusive and aggressive behaviour.

M had been seen by a number of psychiatrists during his childhood and adolescence. On a recent occasion he had undergone psychometric testing using the Terman-Merrill test and had achieved an Intelligence Quotient of 51. Accordingly, he was considered to be mentally impaired.

M appeared to be severely deaf. He had poor speech and limited verbal language. He had some lipreading ability but his poor language limited his understanding using this medium. However, he gave a reasonable account using sign language and, within the limits of his verbal language, by fingerspelling.

M showed no evidence of mental impairment. He was thought to have a personality disorder possibly related to minimal brain dysfunction and also possibly related to poor parenting and delayed maturation. On psychometric testing, using the performance items of the Weschler Adult Intelligence Scale, he achieved an Intelligence Quotient of 114, the scores on the sub-tests being uniformly above average!

Intellectual impairment may not be recognised

The factors responsible for deafness of early onset sometimes cause more widespread brain damage which may give rise to both deafness and disabilities Deafness is, therefore, sometimes associated mental impairment. As both disabilities can interfere with speech and language development it is not uncommon for either the deafness or the disability to be overlooked.

THE PSYCHIATRIC ASSESSMENT ITSELF

Hearing people often seek psychiatric help themselves or are referred by their general practitioners. Few preverbally profoundly deaf people seek psychiatric help themselves and in the majority of instances referrals are instigated by social workers with deaf people (see Tables 2 and 3).

The reasons why most deaf people do not seek help themselves are twofold. The first is that many preverbally deaf people are unaware of the concept of mental disorder and the availability of psychiatric services. (Indeed, many of the deaf people referred have no idea why they are referred). The second is the atypical nature of the problems presented. In the study of 250 patients referred, only two initiated referral themselves. One of these was a middle-aged prelingually profoundly deaf woman who sought the help of the author at a deaf club where he was a member of the management committee, while the other was deafened postlingually. Social workers with deaf people initiate most referrals. When deaf people require help they turn to those workers with whom they can communicate. In the study, over 55% of referrals were initiated by social workers for the deaf (see Table 3).

TABLE 2
Source of referral of 170 patients (Denmark and Eldridge 1969)

Patients	1
Relatives	2
General practitioners	1
Psychiatrists (mental illness)	19
Psychiatrists (mental impairment)	15
Paediatricians	1
Gynaecologists	1
Audiologists	4
Social workers (Ministry of Health)	3
Social workers (hospital)	3
Social workers (for deaf people)	85
Social workers (memtal health)	5
British Deaf Association	2
Royal National Institute for the Deaf	9
National Deaf Childrens' Society	4
North Regional Association for the Deaf	1
Lecturer in Education of the Deaf	1
Teachers of deaf children	7
Psychologists	3
Magistrate (Member of management of society for the deaf)	1
Borstal Aftercare Association	1
Prison medical officer	1
Total	**170**

The psychiatric assessment of deaf people may be similar to that of normally hearing people, but there are often major differences for the following reasons:

TABLE 3
Source of referral of 250 patients (Denmark 1989)

	Initiator	Referring agent
Patients	2	1
Relatives	5	1
General practitioners	3	100
Consultants (various specialties)	56	95
Community physicians	3	6
School medical officers	2	6
Director of social services	1	–
Social workers (generic)	3	1
Social workers with deaf people	159	3
Teachers of deaf children	5	1
Director of education	1	
Psychologist	1	
National Deaf Childrens' Society	–	1
Royal National Institute for the Deaf	6	7
Deaf/Blind Helpers League	1	–
Court	–	14
Solicitor	–	12
Prison medical officer	1	2
Probation officer	1	–
Total	**250**	**250**

1. Assessment may be extremely complex, difficult and
   time-consuming. When patients have serious communication
   problems it may be impossible to make a proper assessment even if
   the psychiatrist has the requisite skills and expertise.

2. The examination of the mental state of many deaf patients cannot
   be undertaken before the examiner has a proper understanding of
   the patient and his background. In addition to the usual
   background history the following factors often have to be taken
   into consideration also:

   • The degree and age of onset of deafness

   • The cause of deafness and any disabilities

   • The presence of deafness in the family

   • The methods of communication of family members.

- The patient's educational history and achievements. In particular it may be important to know the methods of communication used in school.

- The patient's preferred methods of communication and facility in those methods.

Unfortunately, it is sometimes the case that family members are of limited help in giving background information. Parents are sometimes unable to communicate effectively with their deaf children. As a result, while they may be able to give factual information about past events, they may be unable to give any information as to the patient's attitudes, feelings or beliefs. Information from other sources may also be of limited help or of no help at all. Indeed, in some instances it may even be misleading. For example, some teachers of poor achieving deaf children may give unrealistic reports on their progress. A number have admitted that they have done so because to have given completely factual reports would have caused their parents undue distress.

THE METHOD OF APPROACH TO THE PSYCHIATRIC ASSESSMENT OF DEAF PEOPLE

Special psychiatric services for deaf people are not, and indeed are unlikely to be, always available in an emergency. In consequence, deaf people often have to travel long distances to be seen at out-patient clinics. For this reason, and because the psychiatric assessment of some deaf people can be so time-consuming, every effort should be made to complete the assessment in one session. A methodological approach is therefore necessary as follows:

Before the appointment

Referrals to special services come from a variety of sources but it is good practice to obtain the agreement of the patient's general practitioner or of a local psychiatrist if the patient has already seen one. This is not only a good approach because of medical etiquette, but it is also of importance should it becomes necessary to arrange for the patient to have medication from either of these practitioners. Surprisingly, it has been known for local psychiatrists to refuse to refer deaf patients to specialist services, even though they have been unable to communicate with them themselves. This eventuality should not prevent patients from being referred.

It is not good practice to accept referrals by telephone only. They should be followed up by written referrals so that important information can be obtained before the assessment.

As much information as possible should be obtained before the examination. This should include not only a brief account of the presenting problem and the usual background information, but also the degree, cause, age of onset and family history of deafness, the patient's education and achievements, communication modes and competence in those modes.

A comprehensive history of this nature will not only give the examining psychiatrist some idea of the nature of the presenting problem but will also give some indication of the amount of time which will have to be allocated. Unless the information sent with the request for an appointment is comprehensive, a copy of 'A Suggested Format for a Social History' should be sent either to the referring person or to the local social worker with deaf people (see Appendix Three). Once the social history is received, a decision is made as to whether or not additional information such as school reports or hospital records would be helpful. Finally it has to be decided who should attend with the patient. This might be any or all of the following: relatives, social worker, friends or even workmates or employers. The latter may be the only ones who can communicate properly with the deaf person.

The assessment

Unless the patient is to be seen alone by the psychiatrist, and especially in those instances when the referral has been initiated by another person, it may be helpful to confirm or add to the objective history by interviewing one or more of those persons accompanying workers. For example, before confirming the history of the present condition, additional background information may be necessary to confirm such aspects as the cause of deafness, family history of deafness, and educational history including methods of communication employed. Age of onset and degree of deafness are obviously of importance. Some of the factors responsible for deafness, whether it be prenatal or postnatal may cause more widespread brain damage, while some forms of hereditary deafness are associated with other disabling conditions.

When patients are preverbally deaf, the educational history is often of great importance, especially in view of the controversy over methodology in the education of deaf children. It is also important that the psychiatrist keeps an open mind and does not accept other opinions at face value. This is particularly so if the patient has serious communication difficulties.

The form of the examination will depend upon the methods of communication to be used and the type of problem presented. In some cases psychiatric assessment will be easy. Postlingually deafened patients or patients with partial losses of hearing will, in the majority of instances, have good speech and lipreading ability and communication will present no problems. Similarly, there may be no communication difficulties with preverbally profoundly deaf people without speech if they and the examining psychiatrist are fluent in sign language and fingerspelling. Deaf people with poor language will be more difficult to examine, as they will have difficulty with abstract concepts. When patients are preverbally deaf and have poor sign language skills it may be necessary to resort to gesture, mime and drawing.

Some deaf people have serious communication problems, while in other instances they and their families have developed their own idiosyncratic signs. In these instances it may be helpful to have the help of a family member or a co-worker present. The disadvantage is that there will be no confidentiality.

When there are difficulties in understanding, it is good practice to confirm that the examiner knows exactly what the patient is trying to convey. In normal spoken conversation a question, especially if an affirmative answer is expected, is invariably accompanied by a raising of the eyebrows and a nod of the head. When the person being questioned is deaf and the question is not understood he, or she, may either be unable to indicate that they do not understand the question or may not wish to indicate that they do not understand. In either circumstance the question may evoke a nod of the head (the 'nodding syndrome'). The implications of this may not always be of importance but it may have far-reaching and even disastrous consequences. In a clinical setting there is the danger that a deaf person may apparently answer in the affirmative to a leading question regarding abnormal psychic phenomena. Deaf people may, therefore, appear to admit to holding beliefs that they do not hold or to experiencing phenomena that they do not experience. It is good practice, therefore, to confirm by further questioning when a patient has answered in the affirmative by a nod of the head.

The first part of the psychiatrist's assessment must be to confirm the patient's preferred methods of communication and competence in those methods. It may sometimes also be important to enquire further into the patient's verbal ability and intellectual level. Simple tests of literacy and numeracy are usually easy to administer.

When patients are apparently non-communicating or respond to questions with echopraxia, it is often helpful to try simple tests of the understanding of gesture. A few common objects, or pictures of objects, such as a comb, a pen, a handkerchief and a box of matches, are placed before the

patient and he, or she, is asked, by gesture, to identify them. Correct responses
will indicate that the patient has the ability to learn to communicate by sign
language, albeit at a basic level.

It may not be possible to complete a psychiatric assessment in one session.
In that event a decision will have to be made whether to arrange another
appointment or to admit the patient for a period of observation and further
assessment.

It is important, when patients have poor language skills, to ensure that
what they are conveying is not misunderstood.

> EL, a young severely deaf patient with a history of disturbed
> behaviour, had been admitted for a period of assessment and to
> determine whether she could acquire some skills in sign language.
>
> E was of West Indian parentage. She had been born deaf as the result
> of maternal rubella in pregnancy. She was of low birth weight and all
> her developmental milestones had been delayed. She appeared to be
> somewhat microcephalic and in addition to her deafness she had poor
> sight and had a degree of intellectual impairment.
>
> E had been fitted with a binaural aid but at first refused to wear it. She
> had always had temper tantrums. She had been placed in a school for
> deaf children that adopted an oral only approach to communication.
> However, although she attempted to speak, her speech was
> unintelligible. She was illiterate and innumerate. She communicated by
> gesture only.
>
> One day a member of staff reported that she believed that E was
> hallucinated. She had seen her sitting alone in an armchair. She had
> been rocking backwards and forwards, looking concerned. She had her
> right arm raised to the side of her right ear and, with fingers and thumb
> extended, had been opening and shutting her hand by approximating
> the tips of the index finger and the thumb. However, after spending a
> great deal of time with her and after much enquiry it transpired that
> she was talking to herself and ruminating over the fact that a member
> of nursing staff had shouted at her for not making her bed!

CHAPTER FIVE

PSYCHIATRY FOR DEAF PEOPLE
SERVICE ASPECTS

HISTORICAL BACKGROUND

The plight of deaf people in hospitals for the mentally disordered has been recognised by those concerned with their welfare for some considerable time. In 1912 the Second Nordic Deaf–Mute Congress recommended that deaf patients in psychiatric hospitals should be brought together in the same wards, and in 1929 a Danish deaf man named Hansen made a similar recommendation. In the United Kingdom interest was first demonstrated in 1923 when the Royal Association for the Deaf and Dumb, a charitable organisation in the south-east of England, set up a service of hospital visitors to alleviate the isolation of deaf patients. Later, in 1969, the Royal National Institute for the Deaf approached the Medical Research Council proposing research into the special difficulties of deaf people in relation to mental disorder. However, the Council, obviously unaware of the problems, replied: 'It does not seem that there is a case for attempting to set up research as is envisaged which can only lead to the narrower question of the prevention of deafness.'

Although psychiatrists have been interested in the relationship between deafness and mental illness for a long time there were no special services anywhere in the world before 1955, when an out-patient programme was started in New York, under the direction of the late Franz Kallmann, a psychiatrist and geneticist (Rainer and Altschuler 1966). This was followed in 1963 by the opening of the first residential facility for deaf patients in a psychiatric hospital in Rockland State Hospital, New York State. In the same year a similar department was opened in Saint Elizabeth's Hospital, Washington, DC, by Luther Robinson.

About the same time as psychiatric services for deaf people were developing in the USA, they were also beginning in Europe.

The author's interest in deaf people came about because his father was headmaster and his mother the matron of the Liverpool School for the Deaf. The school consisted of a residential unit and a day school. Although teachers of deaf children were trained in purely oral methods of communication, at that time the author's father, the late Frank L. Denmark, adopted a liberal approach. In the classroom children were taught by oral/auditory methods but were allowed to use sign language and fingerspelling outside the classroom. This was contrary to the philosophy of most schools at that time, many of which punished children if they were found using such methods.

The author first came to understand the importance of communication in medicine when he was a medical student in residence at a maternity hospital.

> Late one evening he received a telephone call from another student who was in the labour ward. He requested help with a young deaf woman who was distressed and with whom nobody there could communicate. Attempts to communicate with her by writing had not been successful.

> The patient was a preverbally profoundly deaf young woman who was without speech and had limited verbal language. However, she was fluent in sign language. She was in pain and was very frightened. She did not understand that they were trying to ease her pain by giving her an analgaesic gas by inhalation. Nobody had been able to explain why they kept putting a mask over her face.

> The author introduced himself, explained what was happening and stayed with the patient throughout the delivery. Discussion with the patient afterwards revealed that she had not had any antenatal instruction.

> The second incident occured during a surgical out-patient clinic. A preverbally profoundly deaf middle aged man had been referred with a swelling on the left upper chest. The clerk was a fellow medical student who presented the case to the surgeon and proferred the opinion, correctly, that the patient had a lipoma. The student explained that the patient was deaf and without speech. The response of the surgeon was to tell the patient in writing that his name would be placed on the waiting list for admission and removal of the tumour.

> While the case was being presented the author was surreptitiously communicating with the patient by sign language and it became

evident that he was very apprehensive. 'Will I die?', he asked, using sign language. The surgeon was moving to the next cubicle but was interrupted by the author. The patient's fears were explained. Further discussion and reassurance that the tumour consisted only of fatty tissue and was not malignant resulted in the patient declining to have it removed.

The author's second post in psychiatry was in a large mental hospital of some 3000 patients. Not surprisingly, there were many deaf patients there. What was surprising was that they were not treated together on the same wards but appeared to be separated by design! Of even more concern was the fact that most had been hospitalised for many years, members of staff could not communicate with them, very few ever had visitors and in many cases the diagnosis appeared incorrect. Many were thought to be mentally impaired but there seemed no evidence for such an opinion.

In the early 1960s the author was approached by Dr R.W. Eldridge, then Deputy Medical Officer of Health and Chief School Medical Officer of Lancashire. Dr Eldridge's interest in deafness stemmed from his work with children in schools in Lancashire and, through his membership of the North Regional Association for the Deaf, he became concerned about deaf people in mental hospitals and hospitals for the mentally impaired. It was Dr Eldridge who persuaded the author to take an active interest.

In 1965, following a study of the deaf population of two large mental hospitals in the north of England (Denmark 1966), an out-patient clinic was started at Manchester University. This was followed by the opening of another out-patient clinic in London in 1968 at the National Nose Throat and Ear Hospital under the aegis of the Royal National Institute for the Deaf. In the same year a residential unit was opened at Whittingham Hospital, Preston, Lancashire (Denmark and Eldridge 1969, and Denmark and Warren 1972). Later still, in 1985, an occasional out-patient clinic was started in Belfast, Northern Ireland.

In 1969, Terje Basilier, a Norwegian psychiatrist, began a programme under the aegis of the Norwegian Society for the Deaf in one of their residential facilities, while in Denmark, in 1970, Jorgan Remvig opened a unit in Glostrop Hospital, Copenhagen. It is of interest that the developments in Europe and the USA were all undertaken independently, none of the psychiatrists involved being aware of similar work elsewhere.

THE PRESENT STATE OF SERVICES

Unfortunately, the incidence of mental disorders in the deaf population is not known. This is due to the methodological problems presented, first in studying such a heterogeneous population, and second, in attempting to conduct mental state examinations when some subjects have serious communication difficulties. Nevertheless, better awareness of the psycholinguistic and sociological aspects of some deafness has led to better appreciation of the need for the development of special psychiatric services in a few countries.

Special psychiatric services for deaf people exist in the USA, in Canada, and in some European countries. In the USA there are more than a dozen residential facilities and more out patient services. In Canada, there is an out-patient service based in Toronto. In Europe, residential facilities exist in England, Sweden, Germany and Holland and there is a day facility for deaf patients in Oslo, Norway. In Denmark, deaf patients requiring hospitalisation are admitted to Glostrop Hospital, Copenhagen. There are no facilities exclusively for them but the wards to which they are admitted are staffed by workers who have the requisite skills and expertise.

In England, there are now three hospitals with special departments of mental health for deaf people. The department at Whittingham Hospital was relocated to Prestwich Hospital, Prestwich, Manchester in May 1993. The other two departments are at Springfield Hospital, London and at the Queen Elizabeth Psychiatric Hospital, Birmingham. These three departments are staffed by over 100 workers, over 30 of whom are deaf.

Psychiatric services for mentally impaired deaf people are not covered in this book. Such services are known to exist in the USA, and in this country sporadic attempts have been made to develop such services. Examples include those at Brockhall and Calderstones Hospitals in Lancashire, and Leavesden Hospital in Hertfordshire. However, most of the patients have now been discharged into the community. Some have been 'habilitated' and live in hostels or other types of sheltered accommodation, while others are living independently. Most hospitals for the mentally impaired have become aware of the communication issues and many now use Makaton with deaf patients and with some hearing patients who have communication difficulties.

Apart from the services mentioned above there are no other special psychiatric services for deaf people. Most countries of the world do not have such services and one can only imagine the tragedies that occur daily. Moreover, in those countries where there *are* special services, they are not comprehensive. An example of the desperate plight of some deaf people was brought to light by the Observer newspaper (Meritt 1989) when it reported on a state mental hospital on the Greek island of Leros, one of the Dodecanese islands in the Aegean Sea. This led to a study of the 1179 mentally disordered patients there (Bouras 1992). Hearing problems were found in 88 patients (7%) and, of these, 38 were said to be completely deaf.

Unfortunately, basic mental health services for hearing people are still poor in many countries, as are services for the assessment, alleviation and treatment of deafness. To expect such countries to develop special psychiatric services for deaf people in the near future is, therefore, unrealistic, but it is a goal which we must strive to attain. To this end the author and his long-time friend, Dr Herbert Feuchte, the father of a deaf child and one-time president of the German Association for the Deaf, founded the European Society for Mental Health and Deafness to press for the development of special services in all European countries.

A DEPARTMENT OF PSYCHIATRY FOR DEAF PEOPLE

Workers with deaf people and workers in mental health are sometimes faced with a deaf child or a deaf adult who is disturbed or who does not appear to be 'normal'. In such circumstances they may not know where to turn for help or may be doubtful if a referral to psychiatric services for deaf people is appropriate. The following description of features of the Department of Psychiatry for the Deaf at Whittingham Hospital may be helpful. It is based upon a sample of 250 patients referred to the author (Denmark 1985).

The department adopted a 'therapeutic community' approach to management which involves the patients in decision making. Unfortunately, it was not possible, because of the communication difficulties of some of the patients, to involve them in all the meetings. However, before any decisions regarding management were implemented they were discussed and ratified at the weekly community (patient/staff) meetings.

Referring agencies

Referrals of hearing people to psychiatrists are usually, although not exclusively, made by general practitioners. General practitioners are usually also the initiators of referrals, although the request or suggestion for referral may come from others, for example the patient themselves or relatives.

Early in the development of the services based at Whittingham Hospital, it was thought that it would be of interest to determine the sources of referral and the records of the first 170 patients referred to the author were studied

(Denmark and Eldridge 1969) (see Table 2, p.77). Later, in the sample of 250 patients (Denmark 1985) both the referring agencies and the initiators of the referrals, that is, the persons who suggested referral, were studied (see Table 3, p.78).

Few preverbally profoundly deaf people seek psychiatric help themselves, probably because they are not aware of the concepts of mental health and mental disorder. In the sample of 170 patients, only one patient initiated referral herself. She was a member of a society for deaf people of which the author was a member of the management committee. In the sample of 250 patients only two deaf people initiated their own referrals. (It is of interest that the one general practitioner who referred a patient was a friend of the author, while the gynaecologist lived next door to him!)

The important feature of both studies is that the large majority of referrals made were initiated by social workers with deaf people. In times of stress deaf people usually turn to those with whom they can communicate – often their local social workers. This makes the role of social workers with deaf people a central one and it is vitally important that they are adequately trained, not only in generic social work but also in social work with deaf people. It is essential that they also have training in mental health issues.

The two studies also highlighted the need for all workers in the caring professions to have some understanding of the psycho-linguistic and social problems of deaf people. The increase in referrals by medical practitioners, by general practitioners but particularly by psychiatrists, in the second study is almost certainly a reflection of the better awareness of the presence of services brought about by publications from the department.

The patients

The lack of special psychiatric services for deaf people means that such services have large catchment areas. However, the most outstanding feature of the department is the wide variety of patients referred in terms of their ages, their range and types of deafness or communication disorder, the reasons for their referral and their diagnoses. The causes of deafness and their methods of communication are also of interest.

Place of residence

Although the numbers of deaf people requiring psychiatric assessment or treatment are relatively small, their communication methods often present major problems for regular psychiatric services because they cannot meet their needs. In the study mentioned above, patients were referred from every

Regional Health Authority in England, while 11 came from Scotland, 9 from Wales and 4 were from Northern Ireland (Table 4). One patient was referred from Eire. The dearth of special services was further underlined by the fact that the author has examined deaf people in Belgium and Germany and has had requests to see others in Greece, Malta, Sri Lanka, South Africa and Switzerland.

TABLE 4
250 Referrals – Place of Residence (Health Authorities)

North Western	75
Mersey	30
Yorkshire	14
East Anglia	3
Northern	10
West Midlands	11
South Western	4
Trent	14
South West Thames	10
South East Thames	6
North West Thames	21
North East Thames	16
Wessex	5
Oxford	6
Scotland	11
Wales	9
Northern Ireland	4
Eire	1
Total	**250**

Because special psychiatric services for deaf people are not always readily available, local services will have to be involved when emergencies arise. It is important, therefore, that interpreters (who are sometimes social workers with deaf people), have some understanding of mental health issues and that general psychiatrists have some understanding of the psycholinguistic and social aspects of deafness and know how to use interpreters.

When deaf patients are referred to special psychiatric services they may have to travel long distances to be examined and, if admission is necessary,

admitted at long distances from their homes. When distances are too great
for the patients to be examined and return home on the same day it will be
necessary either to admit them overnight or arrange for accommodation near
to the clinics. (On more than one occasion, patients who have had difficulty
in communicating with their own families and who have been admitted for
overnight stay have been reluctant to leave the department and return home!)

Their ages

Patients of all ages are referred. In the study of 250 patients, the ages ranged
from 4 to 72 years. The majority were children, adolescents and young adults
(see Table 5). The large numbers of young people referred wass probably
due to the usual problems of adolescence and the onset of functional
psychoses. However, many were immature deaf people who had presented
only minor problems at school where they mixed with their peers and where
members of staff made special efforts to communicate with them. However,
difficulties arose when, after leaving school, they entered a world where most
people, and often even their own families, could not communicate effectively
with them.

TABLE 5
Ages of 250 patients referred

0 – 5 years	1
6 – 10	10
11 – 15	25
16 – 20	56
21 – 25	34
26 – 30	33
31 – 35	22
36 – 40	18
41 – 45	9
46 – 50	13
51 – 55	9
56 – 60	7
61 – 65	5
66 – 70	4
71 – 75	1
75 +	3
Total	**250**

Types of deafness or communication disorder

Most patients are preverbally deaf but others are deafened postlingually, in childhood, in adolescence or in adult life. In the study, most were profoundly deaf but others had lesser degrees of deafness (see Table 6).

TABLE 6
Types of deafness in 250 patients

Onset in childhood {	Preverbal profound	188	}
	Preverbal partial	38	234
	Postlingual profound	10	
Onset in adult life {	Profound	8	}
	Partial	2	10
Not deaf			6
Total			**250**

Some patients have serious communication difficulties. In the study, no less than 48 (18%) had no effective means of communication. Some of these were deaf people with disabilities while others were not deaf but had disorders of communication of other aetiology (see Table 7).

TABLE 7
Developmental Disorders of Communication

	Profoundly deaf	Severely deaf	Partially hearing	Not deaf	Total
Mental impairment and cerebral palsy	3	–	–	–	3
Mental impairment	14	1	2	1	18
Mental impairment and educational deprivation	7	1	1	–	9
Autism	4	–	2	1	7
Specific language disorder	2	–	2	2	6
Other	–	1	2	2	5
Total	**30**	**3**	**9**	**6**	**48**

Patients who are both deaf and blind deserve particular mention because of the difficulties they may present in diagnosis and treatment, especially when they have limited verbal language.

Causes of deafness

Psychiatrists working with deaf people need to be aware of the causes of deafness (see Appendix One) because it may be one feature of an inherited syndrome such as in Usher's Disease or Lange Nielson's Syndrome, or it may be associated with other disabilities, for example rubella embryopathy, or deafness may be symptomatic of other pathology.

> GD, a 13-year-old girl, was referred by an audiologist. She had complained of progressive deafness. No cause had been found and it was suggested that her complaint may be 'hysterical' in origin as she was having difficulties with her schooling and in getting off to sleep.
>
> G complained that she was unable to hear properly in her left ear and that this affected her ability to hear properly in class. She invariably slept on her right side, she said, but was frightened when she closed her eyes because she could not hear anything.
>
> Physical examination revealed signs of intracranial pathology. She was referred to a neuro-surgeon for investigation and was found to have a cerebral tumour.

The causes of deafness in the 250 patients referred is shown in Table 8. In 155 (62%) the cause was not known. It is probable that in most of these instances the deafness was hereditary.

Methods of communication

The department was developed to provide access to psychiatric services for preverbally deaf people because they are unable to obtain help from regular services. However, experience has shown that partially deaf and post-lingually deaf people sometimes require special services also.

Table 9 shows the methods of communication used by 250 patients. It does not, however, indicate the competence of the patients in those methods. For example, 38 patients used oral/auditory methods but most of them had considerable difficulty both in understanding and in making themselves understood. Similarly, while many patients were fluent in British Sign Language, a few used idiosyncratic signs only. Surprisingly, no less than 48 patients were unable to communicate in any meaningful way.

TABLE 8
Cause of Deafness

Congenital	Hereditary	Unspecified	21	34	50
		Pendred's syndrome	5		
		Usher's syndrome	5		
		Waardenburg's syndrome	3		
	Syphilis		1		
	Rubella embryopathy		13		
	Rhesus incompatability		2		
Perinatal	Prematurity		1		3
	Anoxia		2		
Postnatal	Hereditary (Refsum's syndrome)		1		36
	Otitis media		2		
	Measles		1		
	Meningitis		29		
	Cerebral tumour		1		
	Trauma		1		
	Presbyacusis		1		
Not known					155
Not deaf					6
Total					**250**

TABLE 9
Methods of communication of 250 patients

Sign language and fingerspelling			124
Oral/aural			38
Combined oral and 'manual' methods			39
Deaf/blind manual alphabet			2
Non-communicating	adults	25	
	children	21	46
Elective mutism			1
Total			**250**

Reason for referral

Most psychiatrists are unable to communicate effectively with deaf people
and it is not surprising that the majority of referrals are for assessment.
Seventy-eight per cent of referrals were made to determine whether or not
they were suffering from mental disorders or from what form of disorder
they were suffering (Table 10). Some patients are referred for treatment. Of
the 197 patients referred for psychiatric assessment, 33 had been charged
with criminal offences.

TABLE 10
Reason for referral

Assessment		
Psychiatric	197	
Communication disorder	29	
Mental	2	
Audiological	1	235
For educational placement	2	
For residential placement	3	
Vocational	1	
Treatment		
Mental illness	5	
Behaviour disorder	3	
Marital problem	1	15
Sexual problems	2	
Alcoholism	1	
Rehabilitation (mental illness)	2	
'Habilitation'	1	
Total	**250**	

Mental health workers with sign language skills have an important part to
play in the assessment and treatment of people with disorders of communication. Twenty-nine patients (3%) were referred with communication
disorders.

Many referrals are unusual.

MS, a 26-year-old Portuguese deaf woman who was living in a
woman's refuge, was referred by a social worker with deaf people with
a request for urgent admission. There was concern that she might be

deported to Portugal and be admitted to a long-term psychiatric institution there.

M's parents had separated before she was born. She lived with her mother until she was two years old when she was rejected by her. She then went to live with her grandparents.

At the age of three years, M was diagnosed as deaf and was accepted at a school for deaf children as a resident pupil. She was said not to be a good scholar and at the age of 13 years was excluded because of behaviour problems. She returned to her grandparents and worked in the fields as a casual labourer. When she was 23 her grandfather died and her grandmother felt she was unable to cope with her. She went to live with a paternal aunt but there were relationship problems and M came to England to live with her father, her step-mother, and their family. There were further problems. Her father described her as immature and given to fantasising. He and the rest of the family had great difficulty in communicating with her.

M was seen with a Portuguese interpreter. She was profoundly deaf and also had severe myopia. She was without speech and appeared to have a poor command of verbal language (Portuguese). She knew a few English words. She communicated by writing, some lipreading and gesture. She complained that her family locked her in her bedroom when they went out and that her father hit her.

M quickly settled and very quickly acquired some skills in sign language. Ophthalmic examination revealed no abnormality and she was prescribed new spectacles. She proved to be a pleasant young woman but was extremely immature. However, she was eager to learn. She was involved in various programmes including education, occupational therapy and group therapy. She made good progress.

After some months M was transferred to a Rehabilitation Centre for young deaf people where she made further progress. She obtained British citizenship and eventually married a deaf man.

Diagnosis

The 250 patients fell into three main diagnostic groups: (1) those with mental disorders, (2) those with problems related to deafness, and (3) those with developmental disorders of communication (Table 11).

TABLE 11
Diagnosis of 250 patients

Mental disorder	Neurosis and personality disorder	26	
	Schizophrenia	56	
	Affective illness	14	104
	Schizo-affective illness	1	
	Organic reaction	4	
	Other	3	
Problems related to deafness		58	
Developmental disorders of communication		48	
Organic illness		2	
No psychiatric abnormality		9	
Miscellaneous		8	
No final diagnosis		21	
Total		**250**	

MENTAL ILLNESS

One hundred and four patients were diagnosed as suffering from *mental illness*. The commonest illness was schizophrenia. Most of them had been ill for some considerable time but the nature of their disorder had remained undetected. It seems that the signs and symptoms of schizophrenia had not been recognised in the early stages and that the concept of affective disorders is not fully understood by many social workers with deaf people.

TABLE 12
Problems Related to Deafness

Behaviour and adjustment problems	53
Depression due to acquired deafness	3
Alcoholism due to acquired deafness	1
Tinnitus	1
Total	**58**

PROBLEMS RELATED TO DEAFNESS

Fifty-eight patients had *problems related to their deafness.* Three of these had depressive reactions due to the onset of deafness. One became alcoholic following the onset of deafness and one patient was referred with tinnitus. The majority, 53 patients, presented with behaviour and adjustment problems which in the majority of instances were due to maturationally delay (Table 12). It is often difficult to know whether preverbally deaf people who present with problems of behaviour and adjustment have a personality disorder *per se* or whether those problems are the result of immaturity consequent upon deprivation of language and experience. In Table 12 a judgment was made on the basis of the history and presentation. It is probably significant that some of them had disabilities, albeit minor ones. Nevertheless, the large majority had poor sign language skills as well as poor verbal language which were the result of lack of exposure to sign language in their early years.

The desperate plight of some parents was often highlighted when they had to ask members of staff to act as interpreters in order to communicate with their children. One father of a 22-year-old patient asked the author to tell his son that he loved him because he had never been able to do so himself!

COMMUNICATION DISORDERS

Forty-eight patients presented with *communication disorders.* Most of these were deaf children with disabilities while others had developmental disorders of communication of other aetiology (see Table 7).

ORGANIC DISEASES

Two patients had *organic disease.* The case histories on pages 46 (DB) and 72 (LA) illustrate the importance of communication between doctor and patient in all branches of medicine.

NO DIAGNOSIS

It was not possible to make a diagnosis in 21 cases.

REFERRAL BY LAW ENFORCEMENT AGENCIES

Nineteen deaf people were referred by the law enforcement agencies for opinion as to whether or not they were suffering from mental disorder. In nine of these cases no psychiatric abnormality was detected.

Admissions

Of 250 patients referred, 124 (50%) were admitted. Compared to psychiatric services for the hearing population this percentage is extremely high. The main reason for this is that many patients live at considerable distances from clinics and so cannot be assessed and treated on an out-patient basis.

TABLE 13

124 Admissions Status (Section)[*]

	Mental Health Act 1959	Mental Health Act 1983	Number
Informal	5		109
Detained	29 25 26 60	4 2 3 37	 5 4 6
Total			124

[*] All the patients in the sample were admitted to the department under the Mental Health Act 1959. The table also shows the equivalent sections under the Mental Act 1983.

Most patients are admitted informally while some are detained under the Mental Health Act (Table 13). All patients who are detained under the Mental Health Act 1983 must be informed of their rights in relation both to their detention and their treatment. Patients who have communication difficulties are vulnerable and special efforts need to be made to ensure that they are properly informed at all times.

It is difficult to quantify the benefits that accrue from special psychiatric services for deaf people. Untold distress has certainly been prevented by arriving at a correct diagnosis and giving appropriate treatment. An objective indication of the benefits of the service can be seen in Table 14 which shows the place of residence of 124 patients before admission and the place of residence to which they were discharged.

Table 14
Place of residence before admission and after discharge
(124 Admissions of 250 Referrals)

	Admitted From	Discharged To
Home	76	87
Rehabilitation centre for deaf people	–	1
Psychiatric hospital	23	5
Hospital for mentally impaired people	5	4
Special hospital	5	–
Hostel for deaf people	5	17
Hostel for mentally impaired people	3	4
Hostel for physically disabled people	1	–
Hostel – unspecified	3	4
School for deaf children	1	1
Prison	1	–
Children's home	1	1
Total	124	124

Functions

The dearth of special services, the fact that patients have different types of deafness or have other communication disorders, and because they present with such diverse problems means that the department has a number of functions. It also means that staff require special expertise and skills and that special facilities are needed.

Assessment and treatment

The main functions of the department are the assessment and treatment of deaf people with mental disorders. There are only three units in the country providing special psychiatric services for deaf people. Accordingly, some patients live at long distances from the unit and its associated out-patient clinics (see Table 4, p.89). There is often a long waiting time for admission and so assessment is probably the most important function. For example, local services often do not know whether or not a deaf person is mentally disordered and an opinion will often be of great value even if the individual cannot be admitted immediately. In such cases an opinion may enable a deaf person to be managed or treated locally with input from an interpreter or a social worker with deaf people.

The treatment of mental disorders does not come within the scope of this book. However, the treatment of patients who have communication disorders and those with problems of behaviour and adjustment deserve mention.

It has become apparent that some people with communication disorders of varied aetiology can learn to communicate, albeit at a basic level, by using sign systems including British Sign Language. The development of Makaton, a sign system for mentally impaired persons with communication problems has been of immense benefit to many.

Some young, and other not so young, deaf people present with problems of behaviour and adjustment. In many instances their problems are due to immaturity consequent upon impoverished experience. Many of these young people and their parents have not been given the opportunity to learn British Sign Language, which is so vital for proper emotional and social development in the early formative years and for learning. Treatment programmes such as the teaching of British Sign Language, formal education, individual and group therapy, occupational therapy and art therapy in their various forms, and speech therapy where appropriate, can often bring about significant changes even in the relatively short term and facilitate the process of habilitation which may continue after discharge.

It is apparent that programmes of parent counselling with more realistic parent guidance and the early use of sign language have important implications in terms of preventive mental health.

Education and training

Most workers in the caring professions will at some time meet a deaf person who they suspect may be mentally disordered. It is, unfortunately, unrealistic to expect that all deaf people will have access to special psychiatric services in times of emergency. It is important, therefore, that care workers have some understanding of the psycho-social aspects of different types of deafness and know how to get advice or help. It is also important that workers with deaf people, but especially social workers with deaf people and interpreters, have some understanding of mental health issues. One visitor expressed the view that education and training were, perhaps, the most important function of the department. Lectures, seminars and workshops are held and workers of all disciplines are accepted for training.

Research and publications

The staff of a department of psychiatry for deaf people have a responsibility to share their knowledge and experiences with other workers. The recent acceptance of the need for sign language in the education of deaf children and the development of special psychiatric services in this and other countries have derived in no small part from the research and publications of staff in this and similar services.

STAFFING

The communication difficulties of many of the patients and the variety and atypical nature of the problems presented require staff from a number of different disciplines with special skills and experience. It is of fundamental importance that staff members should have in-depth understanding of the psychosocial implications of different types of deafness and of communication disorders, both developmental and acquired. They must be conversant with mental health issues and the Mental Health Act 1983 and be fluent in sign language and in fingerspelling. Almost as important as the knowledge and skills required are the attitudes and personalities of the staff – their tolerance and patience and their ability to empathise.

It is particularly important that there are deaf members of staff, so that a non-disablist and culturally sensitive service can be provided. Deaf members of staff also act as role models for immature deaf patients.

Few hearing people acquire the skills in sign language to compare with deaf people whose first language is sign language. Deaf members of staff will, therefore, often be able to communicate more easily with preverbally deaf patients, especially those who have limited ability to communicate in any medium or who use idiosyncratic sign language. They can help new members of staff without direct experience of deafness to understand the psychosocial implications of deafness and deaf culture. They will also act as advocates for patients.

Whenever possible, members of staff should be deaf. At the time of writing there are 13 deaf members of staff at the National Centre for Mental Health and Deafness at Prestwich Hospital.

The differences in communication modes and the competence of different patients in those modes means that a high staff/patient ratio is necessary. Some patients, for example those who are both deaf and blind, need to be given information on an individual basis.

Psychiatrists require the special skills and expertise mentioned earlier in this book. It has, understandably, proved particularly difficult to find psychiatrists to undertake further training after many years as undergraduates and then as postgraduates. The necessary motivation often results from acquaintance with deaf people either at first or second hand.

The shortage of psychiatrists working with deaf people means that they are asked to see deaf people of all ages – children, adolescents and adults, with different types of deafness and presenting with a variety of different problems. It follows that they must have both a wide range of special skills and experience. Newcomers to this very specialised sub-specialty must be aware that no sooner do they start working with deaf people, they will be immediately recognised as specialists in that field.

The stressful nature of psychiatric nursing is recognised by the General Nursing Council. When patients have communication differences in addition, psychiatric nursing becomes even more stressful and difficult. Some patients have communication difficulties of such a degree that it may be extremely difficult or even impossible to understand them or be understood in spite of fluency in sign language and English.

The communication modes and competencies in those modes often differ greatly from patient to patient. It is not only difficult, therefore, to obtain the attention of a number of deaf patients at the same time, simply because they cannot be called to attention by audible methods, but it is often necessary to explain issues or give information to some patients individually.

Mentally disordered deaf patients may become disturbed and physical 'acting out' is not uncommon. Nursing staff must not only understand the reason for such behavior but may have to intervene. When approaching disturbed patients who are normally hearing, it is possible to try to reassure and to explain by speaking to them in a calm and reassuring way. In the case of disturbed deaf patients this will not be possible unless there is good eye contact. Moreover, if staff do not have the communication skills to understand the situation and to try to defuse it, they will feel impotent. In such situations, and because of the need to take some action, they may adopt an authoritarian stance and use too much force.

The nursing of mentally disordered patient who are deaf or who have communication disorders of other aetiology requires not only that nurses have personal qualities of a high order, but also special expertise and skills.

In addition to the usual disciplines of psychiatry, nursing, psychology and occupational therapy, the department required other workers. A speech and language therapist was involved in the assessment and treatment of patients with speech and/or language disorders.

Many of the patients with behaviour and adjustment problems have poor communication skills and limited educational achievements. Not surprisingly, their social skills are often poorly developed and some are only be able to manage in the community with a great deal of support. The department employed teachers who tailored to the needs of each patient.

Most patients with poor sign language skills benefited from the continual exposure to this British Sign Language. Others required individual teaching in British Sign Language or Makaton. Some patients needed help with numeracy, literacy and general knowledge. Subjects such as budgeting, sexuality, pregnancy and childbirth, marital and parental responsibilities and aspects of civil and criminal law had to be taught to some patients.

Art therapy and drama therapy are often helpful in assessing patients with communication difficulties. In its various forms, art is a most useful therapeutic tool. For some patients, new experiences in art may be the first occasion on which they have achieved success.

FACILITIES

The psychiatric service for deaf people began as an out-patient clinic in 1965 but it soon became apparent that an in-patient facility was necessary if proper assessment and treatment was to take place. In 1968 the residential department at Whittingham Hospital, Preston, Lancashire, a large psychiatric hospital, was opened. At that time there was little understanding of the problems faced by deaf people or of the need for special mental health services. Indeed, at that time the National Deaf Children's Society was opposed to the use of sign language in the education of deaf children, while the Royal National Institute for the Deaf had not formulated a policy in that respect.

Until 1967 the author had worked in a psychiatric unit in a general hospital, but accepted an appointment at Whittingham Hospital on the understanding that a ward would be made available for a deaf unit (Denmark and Warren 1972). The ward designated had housed 50 long-stay male patients. With grants of £500 from both the British Deaf Association and the Royal National Institute for the Deaf, minor alterations were made and the ward was redecorated. The unit consisted of twelve beds for each sex with accommodation for up to six day patients. Gradually, more funds were made available and the facilities expanded.

The department at Whittingham Hospital was developed on a shoe-string budget when the need for special psychiatric services for deaf people was little appreciated. However, social workers with deaf people soon became aware of the existence of the service and before long demands for the service were such that the waiting time for new patients to be seen at the monthly out-patient clinic at the National Nose Throat and Ear Hospital, London was over two years and the waiting time for the admission of male patients was over twelve months. The development of two other departments, one at Springfield Hospital, London in 1975 and another (Denmark House) at the Queen Elizabeth Psychiatric Hospital, Birmingham in 1993, have lightened the burden and provided reasonable access to services for many more deaf people.

The need for a better department, the development of community care, and the planned closure of Whittingham Hospital, led to the relocation of the department to a purpose built unit, the National Centre for Mental Health and Deafness (the John Denmark Unit), at Prestwich Hospital[*], Manchester in May 1993.

Some of the benefits of special psychiatric services for deaf people are obvious. Others are less apparent. The acceptance of the need for sign language in the preschool years as well as in formal education have, in no small part been due to workers in the field of mental health and deafness. Another is the greater awareness of both lay people and professionals of the special problems, needs and rights of deaf people who are mentally disordered. However, there is still a long way to go.

Few countries have special psychiatric services for deaf people and in those countries that have them they are not comprehensive. Many long-stay deaf patients remain isolated in mental hospitals and there are very limited forensic psychiatric services for deaf people.

---

[*]   Now the Mental Health Services of Salford NHS Trust

CHAPTER SIX

MENTAL HEALTH LEGISLATION AND DEAF PEOPLE

THE MENTAL HEALTH ACT 1983

Admission and treatment

The laws in relation to the admission and treatment of mentally disordered people differ from country to country and are often changed from time to time. Before 1959, admission and treatment in England and Wales were governed by the Lunacy Act of 1890 and the Mental Deficiency Act of 1913. Under these Acts, mentally disordered people were admitted to hospital either as voluntary patients or against their wishes under certification. Voluntary patients had to indicate their agreement to admission by signing a form to that effect and they had to give written notice of their intention to leave hospital.

The Mental Health Act 1959 not only enabled patients to enter hospital informally in the same way that physically ill patients are admitted to general hospitals but it also allowed the admission of patients who were not volitional on an informal basis. The 1959 Act also did away with certification by magistrates so that compulsory admission became a medical matter. Appeals against formal detention were also allowed.

In the 1960s and the 1970s there were a number of enquiries into standards of treatment and care of patients both in mental hospitals and hospitals for the mentally impaired. These raised interest of such bodies as Mind, the Council for Civil Liberties and the British Association of Social Workers and led to a new Mental Health Act in England and Wales in 1983. This Act made further provision to safeguard patients' interests. It also served as a stimulus to individuals and institutions concerned with deaf people to look into their rights not only in relation to admission and detention but also to treatment.

The British Deaf Association in particular has for a long time been concerned with the rights of deaf people and requested Parliament that special provision be made within the new Act for deaf patients when admitted for assessment or treatment. This proposal was accepted and Section 13 of the Act requires approved social workers to interview patients 'in a suitable manner'. This phrase was more fully explained in a Memorandum to the Act circulated to all Social Service Departments in 1987 which referred to the need to 'take into account any hearing or linguistic difficulties the patient may have' (paragraph 38) and that the giving of information by hospital managers orally and in writing may not be sufficient (paragraph 276). However, it was not until the Code of Practice was published in 1990 that the particular difficulties of some deaf people were addressed. The main recommendations are as follows:

1. Where the patient has difficulty either in hearing or speaking, wherever practicable an approved social worker with appropriate communication skills should carry out the assessment or assist the approved social worker assigned to the case. Alternatively, the approved social worker should seek the assistance of a professional interpreter. Social service departments should issue guidance to their approved social workers as to where such assistance can be obtained.

2. The patient's cultural background should be considered.

3. Where the patient and the doctor cannot understand each other's language the doctor should have recourse to a professional interpreter, who understands the terminology and conduct of a psychiatric interview (and if possible the patient's cultural background).

4. Doctors should receive guidance from local authorities on the use of interpreters and there should be arrangements for their easy access.

5. When conveying information to hearing-impaired patients, hospital managers are advised that assistance should be sought from social workers with deaf people and advice from the British Deaf Association or the Royal National Institute for Deaf People.

DB, a 72-year-old preverbally profoundly deaf man, was referred by a psychiatrist at the suggestion of a social worker with deaf people. He had been admitted informally to the psychiatric unit of a general hospital three weeks previously, apparently following complaints from his wife about his behaviour.

The story obtained from the patient and the social worker who accompanied him to see the author at an out-patient appointment was as follows. He had been born deaf and had been educated at a school for deaf children. After leaving school he had been employed as a boot repairer and then a factory worker. He had married but his wife died and he then went to live with his sister.

About four years previously, he had been involved in a road traffic accident and had received a large sum of money in compensation. He remarried a much younger deaf woman shortly afterwards mainly, he said, because of loneliness. The money had been put into a joint account at her instigation. The second marriage had never been a happy onem mainly because his wife frequently associated with other men.

Just before D's admission, his wife had complained about his behaviour and had accused him of hitting her. He had been admitted to the psychiatric department of his local hospital as an informal patient.

D appeared to be a pleasant man who, using sign language and fingerspelling, gave a good account. There was no evidence of mental disorder and discussion revealed that he did not know the laws in relation to admission to mental hospital and did not understand the concept of informal admission. He did not know, therefore, that he could have refused admission to hospital and could have left at any time. The situation was explained to him. He agreed to return to the hospital from which he had come until arrangements could be made for him to return to live with his sister. The referring psychiatrist was contacted by telephone. D returned to his parent hospital but was discharged the following day.

There are particular difficulties in relation to the admission and treatment of deaf people who do not have good English language. Special efforts must be made to ensure that competent sign language interpreters are available at every stage of proceedings under the Mental Health Act. Family members should not be employed.

The issue of consent to treatment is of particular importance. Deaf people must be made aware of the purpose and the nature of any treatment envisaged.

Mental Health Review Tribunals

Every person who is admitted against their wishes to a psychiatric department or hospital under a Section of the Mental Health Act, except those admitted for 72 hours as a matter of urgency under Section 4, has the right to appeal for his/her discharge to a Mental Health Review Tribunal. All patients must be informed of their rights in this respect and it is the duty of hospital managers to ensure that any patient who wishes to apply to a Tribunal is given every opportunity and assistance to do so. This includes the right to legal representation.

It is important that Mental Health Review Tribunals involving deaf patients are conducted in a suitable manner. Ideally, the medical members of such Tribunals and independent psychiatrists examining deaf patients should have the requisite communication skills and expertise to examine patients alone. When such psychiatrists are not available, interpreters need to be employed. Ideally, these should not only be fluent sign language interpreters, but should be conversant with mental health issues.

Even deaf patients in special psychiatric units for deaf people will be disadvantaged unless proper arrangements are made. Mental Health Review Tribunals involving deaf patients should be wholly independent and members of the unit staff should not be used as interpreters. Solicitors acting on behalf of deaf people in respect of Mental Health Review Tribunals need to be 'deaf aware'.

Whenever there are any difficulties in respect of mental health legislation, the advice of a specialist social worker for deaf people should be sought. If, for any reason, there are difficulties in this respect, help can be obtained from the Royal National Institute for Deaf People or the British Deaf Association or any of the three special departments of psychiatry for deaf people (see Appendix Three).

THE COURT OF PROTECTION

Mental illness or mental impairment may be of such a nature or degree to render people incapable of managing their affairs. When that is the case they are prone to exploitation and their affairs should be protected by referral to the Court of Protection, an office of the Supreme Court.[*]

---

[*]   Stewart House, 24 Kingsway, London WC2B 6HD.

For a person's property and affairs to be administered by the Court it must be satisfied that the person's incapacity is due to mental disorder within the meaning of the Mental Health Act 1983.

When it is considered that a person is incapable of managing their property and affairs, a responsible person should make application to the Court. The Court will then consider medical evidence and, if it is satisfied that the person is incapable, it will arrange for their affairs to be managed for them. The usual method of doing this is to appoint a Receiver who is usually a relative but may be another person such as a Director of Social Services. The Court will make an order giving the Receiver powers to administer the person's property and affairs, but under specific conditions stipulated by the Court.

Deaf people who are mentally ill or mentally impaired may be unable to manage their affairs. However, there are probably a considerable number of deaf people who are not capable of managing their affairs and are vulnerable to exploitation, who are not recognised as being incapable. In most instances they are mentally impaired but this has not been recognised because their poor social functioning has been attributed to their deafness.

Both hearing and deaf people may appear to be capable of managing their financial affairs when they are not. For example, it is not uncommon when questioning care workers about their clients to be told that they can manipulate money, simply because they are known to purchase goods from shops. However, further enquiry will sometimes demonstrate that they do not know whether or not they have been charged the correct amount or received the correct change.

In all instances where it is suspected that a person might be incapable of managing their affairs, they should be assessed by competent workers, and the help of a solicitor should be sought with a view to referral to the Court of Protection. All professionals working with deaf people have a responsibility to safeguard the interests of their clients in this respect.

> JR, a single lady of 53 years of age, was referred by a social worker with deaf people. He requested an assessment as he was concerned that she may not be capable of managing her affairs which were being dealt with by a solicitor, and also to discuss her residential placement, as she was living in a homeless family unit.

> J was apparently a normal child at birth but contracted meningitis at the age of eight months. Her developmental milestones were somewhat delayed thereafter and she did not walk until she was three years old. She started school at six years and made slow progress. However, it was

not until she was ten years old that a hearing impairment was diagnosed.

J left school at the age of 16 and then attended an Assessment Centre which recommended domestic work. She held a number of such posts. Following the death of her parents her affairs were placed in the care of the family solicitor. The family home was sold and J was placed in various hostels and then in homeless accommodation.

J presented as a pleasant, anxious severely deaf woman of low-average intelligence. Her speech was intelligible and she was able to lipread reasonably well in a one-to-one situation. She gave a reasonable account of her past history but was unaware of the extent of her savings, which were considerable. She had a rough idea of the amounts of money that she had in two bank accounts but had no idea how much she had in a third one. She had deposits in five different building societies, but had no idea how much she had in any of them. She was not happy with her solicitor and wished to find another one. Subsequent psychometric assessment indicated that she had a degree of mental impairment. It was recommended that J's affairs should be placed in the hands of the Court of Protection.

J was found accommodation in a hostel. She settled well in her new accommodation, At a later date she decided that she wanted to make a will. At the request of the Master of the Court of Protection this was witnessed by the author. Her living relatives had had no contact with her for many years and she decided to bequeath her money to two charities – one for deaf people and the other for the mentally impaired. She recalled that a girl with Down's syndrome used to live next door when she was a child.

ADVOCACY

Advocacy, the process of acting on behalf of other people, arose out of the civil rights movement in the USA in the 1960s. Advocacy agencies are now common throughout Europe and are particularly relevant to people with disabilities.

In the UK, a number of national bodies, including the National Association for Mental Health and the King's Hospital Fund, have become involved in the provision of advocacy for patients in mental hospitals. There is no group of patients who are more in need of advocacy than patients in mental hospitals, both those admitted informally and those who are detained against their wishes, who have communication problems with members of staff. Perhaps the most common and most important of these are preverbally deaf people with limited verbal language. Social workers with deaf people have special responsibilities in this respect. Should hospitals have any difficulties, they should contact the Royal National Institute for Deaf People or the British Deaf Association (see Appendix Two).

CHAPTER SEVEN

CRIME AND DEAF PEOPLE

INTRODUCTION

There are so few psychiatrists specialising in working with deaf people that they need experience in many subspecialties. One of these is forensic psychiatry. In a sample of 250 patients referred to the author (Denmark 1985), 33 had been charged with criminal offences.

Crimes are committed against deaf people and crimes are committed by deaf people.

CRIMES AGAINST DEAF PEOPLE

Both deaf children and deaf adults may be the victims of crime simply because they are deaf.

Physical, sexual and emotional abuse and neglect

In recent years it has become apparent that the prevalence of child abuse, emotional, physical and sexual, and neglect, are far more common than was previously thought. Workers in the field of deafness have long been concerned that deaf children are particularly vulnerable to abuse both by their relatives and by caring staff in residential establishments. This problem has been highlighted both in this country and in the USA. Of 156 returns of questionnaires to teachers of deaf children and social workers for deaf people, 86 (55%) reported incidents of physical and emotional abuse and 50 (32%) of sexual abuse (Kennedy 1988), while in a survey of 100 deaf people in the north west of England, over 50% of deaf adults reported incidents of abuse, both physical and sexual (Ridgeway 1993, unpublished research).

There are probably a number of reasons why there is a high incidence of deaf children being sexually abused. The abuser may believe that the deaf child would not be able to complain or would be unaware that such behaviour is unlawful. The deaf child may not have sufficient sexual awareness, or may be overdependent on others. One young deaf female patient was the object of incest by her father from the age of seven years until, at the age of twelve years, she learned that such behaviour was against the law. Another deaf female was sexually abused between the ages of 15 and 24 years. At the age of 27 years she learned of the concept of sexual abuse on a subtitled video programme on the television (Ridgeway 1993, unpublished research).

Not only deaf children, but deaf adolescents and even young deaf adults, especially those who are poorly educated, may not be aware that abuse is an offence in law and are, therefore, vulnerable.

Everyone involved in the care of deaf children and vulnerable deaf adults – parents, teachers, social workers with deaf people and residential care workers – must be alert to the possibility of emotional, physical and sexual abuse and neglect.

Exploitation

Poorly educated and socially immature deaf people may be the victims of exploitation by unscrupulous people with regard to their financial affairs and sometimes their property. Social workers with deaf people should be vigilant in this respect. Whenever there are issues of competence, consent or testamentary capacity, the deaf person should be assessed by a psychologist or a psychiatrist with the relevant expertise and skills.

CRIMES COMMITTED BY DEAF PEOPLE

Prevalence

Some poorly educated and socially immature deaf people commit offences because of ignorance of the law. Others are easily persuaded and may become the dupes of hearing criminals. However, it is also true that criminal proceedings against deaf people may fail to be instituted or may be stopped inappropriately. When a deaf person is suspected of a minor crime and apprehended he may not be arrested, either out of sympathy or because the communication problems make arrest difficult, or both. Moreover, some social workers with deaf people will attempt to persuade the law enforcement agencies not to prosecute. Defence lawyers often adopt similar attitudes.

The true prevalence of criminality amongst deaf people is, therefore, difficult to determine.

Types of crime

There has not been any satisfactory research to determine whether deafness predisposes to any particular type of crime. Most studies have commented upon the frequency of immaturity and impulsivity amongst deaf offenders but these are common characteristics of hearing offenders also. It seems possible, however, that deaf people are more likely to commit offences against the person, both physical and sexual, than are hearing people (Denmark and Skelton 1976, unpublished research, and Klaber and Falek 1963). This may be because of the difficulties of some deaf people in being able to express their feelings when with hearing people, and sexual frustration because of limited opportunity for relationships with members of the opposite sex on the other. In the study of 250 patients referred to the author (Denmark 1985), 33 had been charged with criminal offences. Of these the majority, 18 (56%), had been charged with offences against the person, of which 11 were sexual offences.

Criminal proceedings

Effective communication is essential throughout every stage of criminal proceedings, from apprehension to sentencing.

Apprehension, arrest and charging

Members of the law enforcement agencies should have some basic understanding of the communication skills required to communicate with people with different types of deafness. This applies particularly to the police, because it is they who are likely to be suddenly faced with a deaf person with serious communication difficulties. Should further action be taken, for example the involvement of solicitors or the courts, it is likely that social workers with deaf people or other advocates will be involved. The involvement of professional workers and interpreters is important at this stage particularly, because the deaf person may not be aware of his rights. With this in view and following the Police and Criminal Evidence Act (1984), the Home Secretary issued Codes of Practice applicable to 'special groups, which include deaf people, and the Home Office produced Circular No 88/1985 on the aforementioned Act. The Codes of Practice and the Circular stress the importance of having an interpreter present when being questioned or charged. Unfortunately, at present there are no strict rules regarding the competence of interpreters, although most courts now expect them to be registered on the list of the Council for the Advancement of Communication with Deaf People.

In 1953 a preverbally profoundly deaf man was charged with murder in the presence of an interpreter. To the charge, he is reputed to have replied 'Yes, I understand'. However, a Missioner for the Deaf who became involved in the case found great difficulty in communicating with the man and came to the conclusion that he would not be capable of following court proceedings. At the trial, another interpreter was sworn in but he also was of that opinion. Accordingly, he informed the court that it would not be possible to interpret the proceedings. Surprisingly, the case proceeded without interpretation. However, the only evidence against the accused was that he had been seen in the vicinity of the house where the crime was committed on the day of the crime and that he had, according to the first interpreter, admitted to having committed the offence when charged. He was found not guilty and released.

Court Proceedings

It is important that courts are made aware of the communication modes of deaf people and that in some instances they have serious communication problems. Interpreters should meet defendants before the proceedings to determine their preferred methods of communication and their facility in those methods. Any particular difficulties should be made known to the court before proceedings begin. Moreover, they should proceed at a pace which allows proper interpretation of the proceedings to take place. Unfortunately, it appears that at present interpreters often do not meet their clients before proceedings start. 'We just do our best', commented one social worker with deaf people who frequently acts as an interpreter. This cannot be in the best interests of some deaf defendants.

FITNESS TO PLEAD

Until relatively recently deaf people without speech were, in many countries of the world, regarded as legally incompetent and unfit to stand trial. However, today most, but not all, countries afford deaf people their privileges and rights and hold them responsible for their actions.

For a long time it has been a generally accepted principle of law that a person should not stand trial if he is incapable of following the court proceedings and of making a proper defence. Most people who are unfit to plead are seriously mentally ill or severely mentally impaired. Some people with preverbal profound deafness who have poor sign language skills fall into this category. Until recently the law held that if they were found unfit to plead the only course would be to send them, without trial, to a psychiatric hospital with a restriction order for an indefinite period (Criminal Procedure (Insanity) Act 1964). This unsatisfactory state of affairs recently aroused a great deal of concern as it was feared that such a finding would lead to incarceration in hospital indefinitely. That this was not necessarily so was illustrated by two cases, where, in each case, the defendant had very poor communication skills and was found unfit to plead. The first was treated in hospital and then discharged, while the second was admitted to hospital but discharged by a Mental Health Review Tribunal. Nevertheless, the Butler Committee on Mentally Abnormal Offenders which reported in 1975 suggested that when an accused person was found unfit to plead a trial of the facts should take place. If, as a result, the person was found not guilty he would be discharged, but if guilty the disposal should be a flexible one. This very sensible law has now been enacted by Parliament. Under the new Criminal Procedure (Insanity and Unfitness to Plead) Act 1991, the courts hold a trial of the facts to determine whether or not the defendant committed the offence(s). If found either guilty, or not guilty by reason of insanity, the court can now choose from a range of options. These include a Hospital Order or a Guardianship Order under the Mental Health Act 1983, a supervision order or an absolute discharge.

The question of fitness to plead may be raised by the prosecution or the defence, but it may also be raised by an interpreter.

> CM, ages 32, was referred by the Crown Prosecution Service. He had been charged with gross indecency with a young child and the question had arisen of his fitness to plead.

> C had been born prematurely and was of low birth weight. He was jaundiced at birth, reputedly due to biliary obstruction which required surgery. He was rejected by his mother and was fostered when he was six months old. Later, at the age of eight, he was adopted. His fostering and adoption were in no small part due to the fact that his adoptive mother was employed in a school for deaf children.

> C was assessed at nine months at a University Department of Audiology by the professor in that department. Bilateral deafness was diagnosed and hearing aids were prescribed. According to his parents, he underwent psychological testing at the age of three, and they were

told that he could never be educated. At no time had the question of methods of communication been discussed.

Just before he reached the age of five, C began to attend a school for deaf children which adopted a purely oral approach to communication. He remained at school until the age of 16, after which he received training in bakery in the school's further education department. Shortly after leaving school he stopped wearing his hearing aids.

After leaving school, C was employed as a baker and was working at the time fo the alleged offence. However, because he was unable to manage his own affairs, these were taken over by his parents. C had a good work record. He had no friends. He enjoyed watching television, was an avid supporter of his local football team and enjoyed visitng a local public house. His parents ensured that he never had sufficient money to overindulge in alcohol.

C was of small stature. His gait and movements wer slightly unco-ordinated. He had a slight left-sided facial palsy and slight spasticity of all four limbs. He smiled readily.

C was profoundly deaf in his right ear and severely deaf in his left ear. Although he had some hearing in his left ear, he had very limited auditory verbal language. Using his limited hearing, together with lipreading and gesture, he could understand some spoken language, provided only simple language was used. His speech was poor and would be unintelligible to anyone not used to communicating with deaf people. C understood a few signs and gestures but had no real knowledge of British Sign Language. Both his parents agreed that they could only communicate with him on a very basic level.

C was functionally illiterate. For example, when he was asked to write the names of different parts of the body, he wrote 'armbow' for 'elbow' and 'thump' for 'thumb'. It was not, therefore, possible to communicate with him through fingerspelling or the written word. He had great difficulty in performing even simple arithmetical tasks.

It was only possible to communicate with C on a very superficial level using speech combined with gesture. It was soon evident that it was not possible to explain to C the purpose of the examination, nor did he seem to understand the serious nature of the charge made against him. Even with an expert interpreter, he would be unable to instruct counsel or follow court proceedings.

C was considered to be a severely deaf man with a relatively minor degree of mental impairment and cerebral palsy. His disabilities were probably the result of brain damage due to neonatal jaundice.

C was found unfit to plead.

Criminal responsibility and sentencing

In the distant past, deaf people without speech were held not to be legally responsible, but nowadays deafness alone is not considered to be a defence. There are, however, certain issues in respect in relation to criminal responsibility and sentencing which are important.

There are particular difficulties in sentencing deaf people, for the alternatives may not be satisfactory. Community service orders and probation orders are often inappropriate because of the communication difficulties and poor general knowledge of some deaf people, although there are three probation offices which have achieved levels of competence in British Sign Language. Custodial sentences often mean that deaf prisoners are deprived of effective interaction with others throughout the whole of their time in prison.

Courts are often unduly lenient towards deaf offenders out of sympathy for them. This, however, may not always be in the best interest either of the offender or of society, for it may leave the offender with the impression that the offence was not serious or that deaf people are invariably treated more leniently than hearing people.

DL, a 23-year-old preverbally profoundly deaf man, was charged with robbery with violence and was referred for psychiatric assessment. He had a previous record of similar offences. On one occasion he had robbed a stranger in a park and had cut his face with a knife. He had been fined or put on probation.

D appeared to be of good intelligence. His first language was sign language and he gave a good account. There was no evidence of mental disorder. Although he knew the author was a doctor he had no concept of mental disorder or of psychiatry.

It soon became apparent that D knew that what he had done was wrong and explained, in sign language, that he intended to plead guilty. When asked what sentence he thought he would receive he replied 'fine or probation'. He was then asked if he thought it was possible that he might go to prison, to which he commented 'Deaf people never go to prison'. Finally, he was asked what was meant by the word 'probation'.

He understood that he had to report to a probation officer on a regular basis but had no idea why. He explained that, in any event, he could not communicate with him. He was found guilty and received a custodial sentence of six months.

Some poorly educated deaf people commit crimes, both civil and criminal, because they are ignorant of the law. The law holds that ignorance is no defence. However, in many instances deaf people are unaware of the law simply because they have not been educated by appropriate methods. In other instances, criminal acts are committed by deaf people who appear to have immature personalities, manifest by impulsivity and aggression. Some of them may have other disabilities, while in other instances their problems may be related to deprivation of experience consequent upon their deafness. In such instances, and especially when deaf people have poor educational achievements, it is difficult to know whether their behaviour is related to their deafness or to other factors. Deaf defendants should be examined by specialists with the necessary skills and experiences. There may sometimes be good reasons to recommend that deaf offenders should be given the benefit of help in 'habilitation' programmes and sentenced accordingly.

Some deaf people who commit criminal acts have mental disorders which are not readily apparent. It is important, therefore, that properly accredited interpreters are used at all stages of criminal proceedings and, should there be any question of mental disorder, deaf defendants should be referred for assessment by a suitably qualified and experienced psychiatrist. Whenever there is any doubt whether a deaf defendant has a mental disorder, he or she should be remanded to one of the three special mental health services for deaf people under Section 35 of the Mental Health act 1983 for a report on his or her mental condition.

CHAPTER EIGHT

SOCIAL WORK WITH DEAF PEOPLE

Social work is that discipline whose members work with the disabled, and with disadvantaged or sick individuals and their families to enable them to function more effectively.

Social work has a relatively short history. For centuries, charitable institutions undertook the work of enabling certain disadvantaged groups to cope more effectively with their problems. Some of these were religious bodies and most were sympathetic towards specific groups. Gradually, the needs of the various groups have become better recognised in most developed countries and much of the work of voluntary bodies has been taken over by social workers employed by local authorities.

The work of the voluntary agencies was mainly concerned with practical help and the provision of opportunities for social intercourse and the term 'welfare worker' came into being. However, as the special problems of different groups became recognised, the need for workers to have special skills was also recognised. This led to the term 'social worker' and the development of special training according to the needs of the particular client group. Moreover, social workers not only provide practical help and support but are expected to provide counselling services both for their clients and their families.

The nineteenth century saw the development of institutes and missions for deaf people. The majority of these were founded by hearing people who were often the children of deaf parents, but sometimes by deaf people themselves. They were established to overcome the isolation of deaf people, but they were often also evangelistic and held religious services. The institutes and missions usually appointed welfare offices and some of these were ordained. The duties of the welfare offices/missioners also came to include interpretation and the finding of employment.

In 1948, the National Assistance Act made it a duty of local authorities to provide social work services for all disabled people including deaf people. Initially, most authorities provided these services indirectly, using existing voluntary services on an agency basis. However, more and more came to provide their own direct services, leaving the voluntary bodies to provide social activities only.

Another milestone in the development of social services was the establishment of a Committee on the Local Authority and Allied Person Social Services, the Seebolm Committee, which reported in 1968. This was set up to rationalise the services, which had become haphazard over the preceding years and had led to much duplication. Undoubtedly, the report led to more efficient services, but its recommendation that all social workers should be generic and work in teams, rather than having specialist workers, was viewed with alarm by many people, not the least by those who were concerned with deaf people. The very fact that many deaf people are only able to communicate effectively by sign language means that generic workers without special skills in communication are unable to fulfil their roles, and so specialist workers are necessary. Fortunately, the need for specialists was soon recognised.

THE ROLE OF THE SOCIAL WORKER WITH DEAF PEOPLE

The role of the social worker with deaf people is in many ways unusual. In times of need deaf people turn to those with whom they can communicate effectively – social workers with deaf people are some of those people. Moreover, not only do they have to provide the usual services of a social worker but they are sometimes called upon to act as interpreters in a variety of settings. Hearing people can readily approach a lawyer, a doctor, an estate agent, a clergyman, or indeed anyone for help or advice. However few hearing professionals have skills in sign language and so direct access is denied to many deaf people. This means that not only must social workers with deaf people be persons of integrity who will act in a wholly professional manner, but also that they must have special training not only in generic social work, but in the special needs of deaf people. Above all, they must have the skills necessary to communicate using a variety of methods, including British sign language, in a variety of situations.

Social workers with deaf people have important roles to play in the field of mental health. They may be called to assess, counsel or to interpret in the case of an emotionally disturbed deaf person, or their opinion may be sought as to whether or not a deaf person is mentally disordered. They may be asked to interpret when a deaf person is admitted to hospital, either informally, or when formally detained under one of the sections of the Mental Health Act 1983. They may be asked to interpret in hospital when a deaf person is being assessed, or when treatment, or their rights under the Act are being explained. They have a responsibility to safeguard the rights of deaf people, especially those who have limited language or are poorly educated. The questions of appeal against detention and consent to treatment are both very important issues. Social workers with deaf people must have a good working knowledge of mental health legislation.

The important role and onerous responsibilities placed upon social workers with deaf people was illustrated in two pieces of research (Denmark 1966, and Denmark 1985). In both of these studies the source of referral to the author was traced. In the first study 50%, and in the second study 55%, of referrals were initiated by social workers with deaf people. They, therefore, have a vital role to play in the detection of mental disorder. Their other important functions are in providing social histories and in supervising and supporting deaf patients and their families in the community.

The following case histories illustrate the important role played by social workers with deaf people and the need for comprehensive training.

> KT, a 54-year-old preverbally profoundly deaf man, was referred by his general practitioner at the suggestion of a social worker with deaf people. The social worker, who had become deaf post-lingually, had good sign language and fingerspelling skills but had not received any formal training in social work. In his referring letter he had written
>
> > For over a year he has had numerous complaints. He has had all his teeth removed, his gall bladder and appendix removed, all without any change. I have tried to choke it out of him but without success.
>
> K communicated well using sign language and fingerspelling. He looked and felt depressed. He had numerous somatic complaints but he also had symptoms of a severe depressive illness, including morning depression, terminal insomnia, anorexia and weight loss. Physical examination showed no abnormality. It was thought that his physical symptoms were hypochondriacal in nature and secondary to a depressive illness. He was admitted to hospital, responded quickly to anti-depressant medication and was discharged symptom-free after six weeks. He was followed up as an out-patient. Medication was gradually withdrawn without any recurrence of symptoms.

꿈 꿈 꿈 꿈 꿈

DM, a 40-year-old single preverbally profoundly deaf man, who lived with his widowed father, was referred by a psychiatrist at the suggestion of a social worker with deaf people. He had been arrested for indecent exposure and threatening behaviour. He had masturbated in the street in front of an old lady and had threatened her with a stick when she challenged him.

D was seen as an out-patient. He had been admitted to a psychiatric hospital some 11 years previously, having become 'agitated, aggressive and with delusions and paranoid ideas'. No diagnosis had been made but he was treated with antipsychotic medication. He gradually improved and his symptoms disappeared. He was seen regularly as an out-patient following his discharge and continued to take medication.

A few months before his referral a new social worker had been appointed. He had just completed his training in working with deaf people. He found D well and sought an interview with the psychiatrist. He told the psychiatrist that he thought that his client's past problems were probably all related to his deafness. The psychiatrist accepted his comments, acknowledging that he had difficulty in communicating with him, and agreed to discontinue the medication. When D reoffended, he readily agreed to the suggestion to refer him to the author.

Prior to the appointment, the social worker sent a social history to which he had added the following comments.

> It seems to me that my client's problems are directly related to his communication difficulties. He is simply lacking in information about life and has seldom the chance to work through his frustration/feelings.

He added that he felt unable to offer sufficient support and sought advice as to how this might be obtained.

D was without speech but had reasonable verbal language and was able to communicate by sign language and fingerspelling. It was often difficult to follow his train of thought and it soon became apparent that this was due to thought disorder of psychotic origin. He had numerous delusions and bizarre ideas. He was hallucinated and had other experiences which appeared analogous to auditory hallucinations. He explained that cars, houses and windows communicated with him. Deaf friends were able to communicate with him in some way although they were not present. They teased him. He believed that one of his workmates wanted to kill him. Sometimes he saw ghosts. When watching the television, females left the screen and annoyed him. His left side told him to do one thing while his right side told him to do another. At times he felt unable to walk. Men and women suddenly appeared in front of him from nowhere. Sometimes they appeared on his shoulder or on his lap. Strangers in the street spoke his thoughts. He could lipread what they were saying.

There was no doubt that D was psychotic and suffering from paranoid schizophrenia. He was admitted to the Department and the medication he had had previously was recommenced. His symptoms quickly disappeared and he was discharged after six weeks with good insight.

Unfortunately, the lack of understanding of the problems of some deaf people not only by the general public by also by many professionals, has been reflected in the poor state of social work services for them. A number of studies have highlighted this (DHSS 1987, RNID 1988, DHSS 1989). These showed that many local authorities employ social workers with deaf people who have had no special training, while other authorities have no social workers with deaf people at all.

Special training for social workers with deaf people has been available in different forms from 1929 onwards. The most recent has been a distance learning course at the Open University which began in 1991. However, funding for this course ends in 1994, so that there will no longer be any formal training for social workers who wish to obtain special training to enable them to work effectively with deaf people and their families.

Social workers with deaf people have to fill many roles. They must not only have generic training but must also understand the psycho-social aspects of different types of deafness. They must also have the communication skills to enable them to communicate with deaf and deaf/blind people and interpret for them in a variety of settings, both informal and formal. Because they are often the only professionals who are able to communicate with them effectively, they have to act as their advocates. They need a good working knowledge of mental health legislation and preferably should have some training in mental health issues. Ideally they should become approved social workers under the Mental Health Act.

EPILOGUE

Until relatively recently there was much ignorance about deafness and deaf people. Only 25 years ago, the management of all deaf children was left to otologists, audiologists and teachers, and sign language was denigrated. At that time the National Deaf Children's Society was dedicated to a strictly oral approach to the education of deaf children (Editorial, *Hearing* 1973) and the Royal National Institute for the Deaf, although not so dedicated to such an approach, did nothing to further the opposite view. Indeed, the Institute has a number of residential facilities for deaf people which have residents whose main, and often only, medium of communication is sign language and yet it did nothing to ensure that the staff were adequately trained in this medium.

In the 1960s, a small number of psychiatrists, psychologists and linguists in the UK, in the USA, in Norway, in Denmark and in Sweden, came to appreciate the need for sign language, not only as a necessary method of communication for the diagnosis and treatment of mental disorders in some deaf people, but also its importance in child development and education. Further developments in the last decade have led to a far better understanding of the psychological, sociological, linguistic and cultural aspects of preverbal deafness. In particular, it has become accepted that sign language is a language in its own right and is the first language of preverbal profoundly deaf people. Unfortunately, there is still a long way to go for some workers with deaf children still do not fully understand the position. For example, one psychologist working with deaf children chose the title 'Psychological aspects of prelingual hearing loss' for a chapter in a book entitled *Deafness* (McKenna 1993). Not only is the word 'loss' inappropriate because many deaf children have never had any hearing, but it tends to minimise their difficulties. Further, he makes no mention of the devastating effects of preverbal profound deafness if steps are not taken to develop meaningful communication between deaf children and their hearing parents in the vital early years.

The development of some counselling programmes for parents of young deaf children and the acceptance of the need for sign language in schools for deaf children has had far-reaching effects in terms of preventive mental health. Where they exist, they have prevented much of the frustration and distress which so commonly occurred when parents and siblings could not communicate effectively with deaf children and have enabled them to develop normally.

The development of special psychiatric services for deaf people in the USA and in some European countries has been of immeasurable importance and has relieved much hidden suffering. It has also led to a better understanding of the difficulties of deaf people by many workers in the caring professions. Much remains to be done. Unfortunately, in some countries the basic needs of deaf people in terms of diagnosis and treatment of hearing problems remain unmet. Some countries, for example, do not have schools or units in regular schools for deaf children. Few textbooks on medicine, nursing, psychology or social work make any mention of the psycho-social aspects of different types of deafness, and yet it would be a relatively simple matter to arrange for every student to attend a lecture to cover the basic facts. Workers should know how to obtain aids to communication and the services of interpreters.

Even in those countries where there are special mental health services for deaf people, problems still exist. There are few, if any, services for the proper treatment of deaf patients requiring long-term treatment in hospital, and forensic psychiatric services are very limited. Many deaf people languish, totally isolated, in prisons and it is likely that many of them would be more appropriately managed in hospitals or other institutions. Mental disorders affect people with all types of deafness but, unfortunately, many deaf people are unaware of the concepts of mental health and mental disorder. However, programmes are now being developed to remedy this situation.

It is hoped that this book will help to further the use of sign language and will enable those care workers who read it to know when and where to get help when they are faced with a child or young person who is deaf, who they suspect may have mental health difficulties. It should be the right of every deaf person to have full and equal access to mental health services which can provide effective assessment and therapy to meet their needs.

Bibliography

Advisory Committee on Services for Hearing Impaired People (1981) *Final Report of the Subcommittee Appointed to Consider Services for Hearing Impaired Children.* London: Department of Health and Social Security.

Alport, A.C. (1927) 'Hereditary familial congenital haemorragic nephritis.' *British Medical Journal.* i:504.

Altshuler, K.Z. (1971) 'Studies on the Deaf. Relevance to Psychiatric Theory.' *American Journal of Psychiatry* 127:1521–1526.

Aristotle. Hist. Anim. IV.

Ashley, Lord J. (1973) *Journey into Silence.* London: Bodley Head.

Basilier, T. (1964) 'The psychic consequences of congenital or early acquired deafness - Some theoretical and clinical considerations.' *Acta Psychiatrica Scandinavica.* Vol 10. Suppl. 180.

Beethoven, L. van. (1802) *Hellingenstadt Document.*

Best, H. (1943) *Deafness and the Deaf in the United States.* New York: Macmillan.

Bettelheim, B. (1990) *Recollections and Reflections.* London: Thames and Hudson.

Bouras, N. *et al.* (1992) 'A needs survey in Leros asylum.' *British Journal of Psychiatry* 161:75–79.

Bulwer, J. (1644) *Chirologia.*

Butler Report (1975) *Report of the Committee on Mentally Abnormal Offenders.* Home Office. Department of Health and Social Security. London: HMSO.

Conrad, R. (1976) *Towards a Definition of Oral Success.* Paper given at the RNID/NDCS Meeting in Harrogate. London: Royal National Institute for the Deaf.

Cooper, A.F., Garside, R.F., and Kay, D.W.K. (1976) 'A comparison of deaf and non-deaf patients with paranoid and affective psychosis.' *British Journal of Psychiatry* 129:532–538.

Criminal Procedure Insanity Act. (1964) London: HMSO.

Criminal Procedure Insanity and Unfitness to Plead Act (1991) London: HMSO.

Critchley, E.M.R., Denmark, J.C., Warren, F. and Wilson, K. (1981) 'Hallucinatory Experiences of Prelingually Profoundly Deaf Schizophrenics.' *British Journal of Psychiatry* 138:30-32.

Denmark J.C, (1966) 'Mental Illness and early profound deafness.' *British Journal of Medical Psychology* 39:117–124.

Denmark, J.C. (1973) 'The Education of Deaf Children.' *Hearing.* Vol 8, No 9. 284–292.

Denmark, J.C. (1985) 'A Study of 250 Patients Referred to a Department of Psychiatry for the Deaf.' *British Journal of Psychiatry.* 146:282–286.

Denmark, J.C. *et al.* (1979) *A Word in Deaf Ears. A Study of Communication and Behaviour in a Sample of 75 Deaf Adolescents.* London: Silverdale Press.

Denmark, J.C. and Eldridge, R.W. (1969) 'Psychiatric services for the deaf.' *Lancet* Aug 2. 259–262.

Denmark, J.C. and Warren F. (1972) 'A psychiatric unit for the deaf.' *British Journal of Psychiatry* 120:423–428.

Department of Health and Social Security (1977) Advisory Committee on Services for Hearing Impaired People. Report of a Subcommittee Appointed to Consider the Role of Social Services in the Care of Deaf People of All Ages.

Editorial (1973) *Hearing* 28:284.

Ewing, A. (1968) In 'The Possible Place of Finger Spelling and Signs.' In *The Education of Deaf Children.* London: Department of Education and Science, HMSO.

Ewing, E. and Ewing, A. (1961) *Your Child's Hearing.* London: The National Deaf Children's Society.

Ewing, E. and Ewing, A. (1964) *Teaching Deaf Children to Talk.* Manchester: Manchester University Press.

Fletcher, C. (1973) *Communication in Medicine.* The Rock Cowling Fellowship. The Nuffield Provincial Hospitals Trust.

Gesell, A. (1956) 'The psychological development of normal and deaf children in the preschool years.' *The Volta Review* 58.117–120.

Gordon, N. (1964) 'The Concept of Central Deafness.' In *The Child Who Does Not Talk.* London: The Spastics Society Medical Education and Information Unit in Association with Heineman (Medical) Books.

Gregory, S. (1976) *The Deaf Child and his Family.* London: Allen and Unwin.

International Research Seminar on the Vocational Rehabilitation of Deaf Persons (1968). Social and Rehabilitation Service. Department of Health, Education and Welfare: Washington, DC.

Ives, L.A. (1967) 'Deafness and the Development of Intelligence. *British Journal of Disorders of Communication.* 2.2:96–111.

Jerval, A., Lange-Nielson, F. (1957) 'Congenital deaf-mutism, functional heart disease with prolongation of the Q-T interval and sudden death.' *American Heart Journal* 54:59–68.

Johnson, S. (1775) *Boswell's account of Johnson's vist to the Braidwood Academy.*

Kanner, L. (1943) Autistic Disturbances of Affective Contact. *Nervous Child* 2:217–250.

Keller, H. (1933) *Helen Keller in Scotland.* London: Methuen.

Kennedy, M. (1988) 'Child Abuse/Sexual Abuse.' *Deafness* 2.5:4–7.

Klaber, M.M. and Falek, A. (1963) 'Delinquency and Crime.' In Rainer, J D., Altschuler, K Z. and Kallmann, F J. (eds) *Family and Mental Health Problems in a Deaf Population.* New York: Department of Medical Genetics, New York State Psychiatric Institute.

Konigsmark, B.W. and Gorlin, R.J. (1976) *Genetic and Metabolic Disorders.* Philadelphia, PA: Saunders.

Kropka, B.T. and Williams C. (1966) 'The Epidemiology of Hearimg Impairment in People with Mental Handicap.' In D. Ellis (ed) *Sensory Impairments in Mental Handicapped People.* London. Croom Helm.

Lane, H. (1976) *L'enfant Sauvage de L'Aveyran.* Paris: Payot.

Lee, H. (1960) *To Kill a Mocking Bird.* London: Heinemann.

Lehmann, R.R. (1954) 'Bilateral Sudden Deafness.' *New York State Journal of Medicine* 54:1481–1488.

Levine, E.S. (1960) *The Psychology of Deafness. Techniques of Appraisal and Rehabilitation.* New York: Columbia University Press.

Levine, E.S. (1960) *The Psychology of Deafness. Techniques of Appraisal for Rehabilitation.* New York: Columbia University Press.

Lunacy Act (1890) London: HMSO.

Martin, J.A.M. *et al.* (1979) *Childhood Deafness in the European Community.* Brussels-Luxembourg: Commission of the European Communities.

McKenna, L. (1993) 'Psychological Aspects of Prelingual Hearing Loss.' In Ballantyne, J. Martin, M.C. and Martin M. (eds) *Deafness,* 243–246. London: Whurr.

McLay, K. and Maran, A.G.D. (1969) 'Deafness and the Klippel-Fiel Syndrome.' *Journal of Lar. otol. 83:175–184.*

Medical Research Council (1969) Reply to the Royal National Institute for the Deaf.

Mental Deficiency Act (1913) London: HMSO.

Mental Health Act (1959) London: HMSO.

Mental Health Act (1983) *Memorandum on Parts I to VI, VIII and X.* London: HMSO.

Mental Health Act (1983) Code of Practice (1990) Dept of Health and Welsh Office. London: HMSO.

Mental Health Act (1983) London: HMSO.

Meritt, J. (1989) Europe's Guilty Secret. *The Observer.* 10th Sept. 1.17.

National Assistance Act (1948) London: HMSO.

National Aural Group (1993) Advertisement.

Pendred, V. (1896) 'Deaf-mutism and goitre.' *Lancet* ii, 532.

Police and Criminal Evidence Act (1984) London: HMSO.

Rainer, J.D. and Altschuler, K.Z. (1966) Comprehensive Mental Health Services for the Deaf. New York: Department of Medical Genetics, New York State Psychiatric Institute.

Refsum, S. (1946) 'Heredopathia Atactic Polyneuritiformis.' *Acta Psychiatrica Scandinavica* Suppl. 38:1–303.

Report of the Proceedings of the International Conference of Teachers of the Deaf held in Milan, Italy in 1890 (1961) London: Allen.

Royal National Institute for the Deaf (1987) 'So Little for So Many.' A Survey of Provision to Hearing Impaired People by Social Service Departments. London: Royal National Institute for the Deaf.

Royal National Institute for the Deaf. (1976) *Methods of Communication Currently Used in the Education of Deaf Children. Papers given at a residential seminar held in 1975.* Letchworth: Garden City Press.

Seebolm Report (1968) Report of the Committee on Local Authorities and Allied Personal Social Services. London: HMSO.

Slater, E. and Roth, M. (1972) *Clinical Psychiatry.* London: Balliere, Tyndall and Cassell.

Social Services Inspectorate, Department of Health and Social Security (1988) Say it Again. Contemporary Social Work Practice with People who are Deaf or Hard of Hearing.

Thomas, A.J. (1981) 'Acquired Deafness and Mental Health.' *British Journal of Medical Psychology* 54:219-222.

Timmermans, L. (1988) *Research Project.* Paper presented at First European Congress on Mental Health and Deafness, Rotterdam, Holland.

Tramer, M. (1934) 'Elective Mutism.' *Kindern Z Kinderpsychiat.* 1:30-35.

Treacher Collins, E. (1900) 'IX Congenital abnormalities: cases 8 & 9 with symmetrical congenital notches in the outer part of each lower lid and defective development of the malar bones.' *Trans.ophthal. Soc. U.K.* 20:190–192.

Usher, R.C.H. (1914) 'On the Interitance of Retinitis Pigmentosa.' *Royal London Ophthalmic Hospital Report.* 19:130.

Waardenberg, P.J. (1951) 'a new syndrome combining developmental abnormalities of the eyelids, eyebrows and nose root with pigmentary defects of the iris and head hair with congenital deafness.' *American Journal of Human Genetics.* 3:195–253.

Warnock Report (1978) Special Educational Needs. Report of the Committee of Enquiry into the Education of Handicapped Children and Young People. London: HMSO.

Wilson, J. (1956) *Language and the Pursuit of Truth.* London: Cambridge University Press.

Worster-Drought, C. (1963) Congenital Auditory Imperception and its Relation to Idioglossia and Allied Speech Defects. *Medical Press* 110:411.

MEANING OF TERMS, CLASSIFICATIONS OF DEAFNESS, CAUSES OF DEAFNESS, and SOME COMMON and SOME IMPORTANT SYNDROMES ASSOCIATED WITH DEAFNESS

MEANING OF TERMS

Some of the terms used by workers with people who are deaf or who have communication disorders have more than one meaning and this can lead to misunderstanding. This problem was highlighted in 1968 during an International Research Seminar in the United States of America. As a result a resolution was passed that 'efforts should be made to develop an internationally agreed terminology relating to the field of hearing impairment'. It also recommended that in the meantime 'prior to future meetings efforts should be made to agree on terminology. Failing this, participants should define their terms of reference before the delivery of papers.' Ives (1967) recommended that workers should define and classify deafness by (a) degree of deafness, (b) age of onset, and (c) the physical origin or site of the lesion.

The meaning of some common terms is explained here. Others are explained under the heading 'Classification of Deafness' which follows. Terms which are used less commonly are to be found in the Glossary. The terminology which relates to mental disorders is that used in the Mental Health Act 1983. In particular, the term MENTAL IMPAIRMENT is used although the term LEARNING DISABILITY is now more commonly used in clinical practice.

Speech

Speech is the communication of verbal language by vocalisation. It is sometimes confused with the word 'language' but the two words have entirely different meanings. For example, parrots can be taught to speak but they have no understanding. (The repetition of speech without understanding is termed 'echolalia'.)

Language

Languages are systems of symbols used for communication. They are usually spoken or written, but the sign systems used by deaf people are forms of language. British Sign Language is the natural language of deaf people in this country. It has its own grammar, syntax and morphology.

Literacy

The word literacy is commonly used to denote ability to read and write. However, with the acceptance of British Sign Language as a language in its own right, with its own grammar, syntax and morphology, the term 'literacy' is now used by some people to denote fluency in sign language also.

Verbal

The term 'verbal' is used with different meanings. It is sometimes used to mean 'by mouth'. It can also mean 'pertaining to words'. It is used in the latter sense in this book. For example, verbal languages are those which employ words and so they can be spoken, written or fingerspelt.

Prelingual, preverbal

The term 'prelingual' has been in common use for many years and is used to describe deafness which is present from birth, or which is acquired before the development of speech and verbal language. However, it is no longer acceptable, because it presupposes that all languages are verbal and this is not the case. The sign languages of deaf people are languages which are non-verbal and yet have their own grammatical rules. It is suggested that the term 'preverbal' is a suitable acceptable alternative term to 'prelingual' and is used throughout this book.

Aural

The word 'aural' pertains to hearing. However, this word, when spoken, cannot be distinguished from the word 'oral' which means by mouth. It is preferable, therefore, when referring to hearing to use the word 'auditory'.

Oral

The word 'oral' means by mouth and must not be confused with the word 'aural' which pertains to hearing (see above).

Deafness, hearing impairment, and the hard of hearing

The terms 'deafness' and 'hearing impairment' are used to describe all degrees and types of deafness, while the term 'hard of hearing' is usually used to describe partial deafness (see below).

CLASSIFICATIONS OF DEAFNESS

Deafness can be classified in a number of ways, using different criteria.

According to age of onset

Congenital
Congenital means 'present at birth'.

Preverbal
The term 'preverbal' is used throughout this book to describe deafness which is present from birth or early age.

Post-lingual
Deafness with onset after the development of speech and language is called 'post-lingual deafness'.

Adventitious
The term 'adventitious' is synonymous with post-lingual deafness.

Presbyacusis
Deafness with onset in later age is called 'presbyacusis'. This is usually associated with the process of aging, but there may be hereditary factors.

According to degree
The British Society of Audiology suggests that deafness should be subdivided into MILD, MODERATE, SEVERE and PROFOUND degrees. However, no classification of degree is entirely satisfactory because the degree of deafness lies on a continuum from a slight loss in one ear to total deafness in both ears. Another problem is that simple definitions do not adequately describe the individual affected. Some people who have lesser degrees of

deafness have considerable difficulty in communicating with hearing people because they have poor verbal language. This can affect their ability to lipread and also the intelligibility of their speech. On the other hand, some people who have severe or even profound deafness may have little difficulty in communicating with hearing people in a one-to-one situation because they have good speech and lipreading ability.

There is, unfortunately, another problem. Some workers use the term 'profound' to describe people whom have little or no hearing when tested audiometrically, even though they may have useful hearing for speech with hearing aids. This can cause much confusion. Children may have little useful hearing for speech on audiometry but may, nevertheless, be enabled to hear and learn to understand speech with a hearing aid. Such children should not be described as 'profoundly' deaf. The misuse of the term 'profound' in this way has helped perpetuate the myth that all deaf children have useful hearing and can learn to speak. The correct criterion should be functional hearing for speech with or without aids to hearing. The benefits of hearing aids can be compared with those of spectacles. Spectacles enable many people with poor sight to see better but do not enable those who are blind to see. Similarly, hearing aids help many people to hear better but they are of no use at all for some deaf people.

The term PARTIAL is commonly used to describe deafness which is not profound and enables the subject to hear and understand speech. However, for this to be possible, all the conditions must be right. There must be good light and clear speech must be used. The term TOTAL is used to mean complete inability to hear sound. Totally deaf people experience the kinaesthetic sensations caused by sound.

The term HARD OF HEARING is commonly used to mean partial deafness. It is of interest that many of the members of the British Association for the Hard of Hearing are profoundly deaf. This Association caters for people who are partially deaf or who have become deaf post-lingually. The common feature is that they communicate by oral methods, in contrast to the British Deaf Association the majority of whose members are prelingually deaf and who communicate by sign language and fingerspelling.

Throughout this book the words 'deaf' and 'deafness' will allude to all degrees of deafness unless otherwise stated.

According to speech intelligibility

The Department of Health requires local authorities to keep registers of disabled people, including those who are deaf. Deaf people are classified as (a) deaf without speech, (b) deaf with speech, and (c) hard of hearing. This is not a satisfactory classification for, although those who are deaf and without speech are usually those whose deafness is preverbal and profound, this is not always the case. The speech of some of those who are deafened post-lingually may deteriorate and become unintelligible, while the speech of many preverbal partially hearing people may be unintelligible also.

According to site of lesion
Conductive deafness

The lesion in conductive deafness is in the auditory canal or in the middle ear. Congenital atresia of the auditory canal, a foreign body, or wax can cause conductive deafness. Malformations of the middle ear, infection (otitis media) and otosclerosis are common causes of conductive deafness.

Perceptive deafness

Perceptive, or sensori-neural deafness, results from lesions affecting the cochlea or the eighth cranial nerve.

CAUSES OF DEAFNESS

The cause of deafness, whether congenital or acquired, is often not apparent. However, there are many recognised causes and these can be classified in different ways. A convenient way is to subdivide them into prenatal, perinatal and postnatal.

Prenatal

Prenatal causes of deafness can be hereditary or non-hereditary.

Hereditary

It is estimated that one child in every thousand is born deaf. In some instances the cause is readily apparent, for example when there is a history of maternal rubella in the first trimester of pregnancy. when there is a family history of congenital deafness or when the deafness is part of a well recognised syndrome. However, in the majority of instances no cause can be found, and it is probable that many of these children have hereditary deafness due to recessive genes.

Most hereditary deafness is congenital, i.e., present at birth, but in other instances the deafness does not appear until later in life. Otosclerosis and Refsum's syndrome are examples of this.

Non-hereditary causes of pre-natal deafness include infections such as rubella in the first trimester of pregnancy, syphilis, and drugs such as thalidomide.

Perinatal

Deafness can be caused in the perinatal period by prematurity, by birth injury or by anoxia. It may also be caused by rhesus incompatibility (kernicterous). In this condition, unborn children have the Rhesus antigen which is absent in the mothers. The mothers produce antibodies which destroy the babies' red blood cells. The cells release bilirubin into the blood stream, causing jaundice. Unless the babies' blood is replaced, the bilirubin is deposited in the cochlea causing sensorineural deafness. Kernicterous may be associated with choreo-athetosis.

Postnatal

There are many postnatal cases of deafness:

- Hypothyroidism: deficiency of thyroid hormone during foetal or early life can cause retarded growth, mental impairment and deafness (cretinism).

- Trauma due to head injury or excessive noise.

- Obstruction of the external auditory meatus by foreign bodies, wax or tumours.

- Tumours of the brain or eighth nerve.

- Infections such as meningitis and cerebral syphilis. (Deafness due to infection of the middle ear, suppurative otitis media, was a common cause of deafness before the discovery of antibiotics. It often resulted in perforation of the eardrum and the discharge of pus from the ear. The sign for 'yellow' before the 1939–45 war in Liverpool used to be the repeated touching of the lobe of the ear by the index finger indicating pus running from the ear.)

- Glue ear or Serous Otitis Media is a sterile effusion in the middle ear which results from incomplete resolution of acute otitis media. It is usually a self-limiting condition.

- Drug toxicity. Many drugs can cause deafness. Examples are streptomycin, kanomycin and neomycin.

- Meniere's disease is characterised by recurrent attacks of vertigo, deafness and tinnitus. Although the hearing improves again after an attack, it tends gradually to deteriorate.

SOME COMMON and SOME IMPORTANT SYNDROMES ASSOCIATED with DEAFNESS

Rubella Syndrome

Infection of pregnant women by the rubella virus in the first trimester of pregnancy can affect the developing foetus in a variety of ways causing visual, hearing, cardiovascular and other defects. Prophylactic immunisation programmes are important.

Pendred's Syndrome (1896)

In this syndrome congenital deafness is associated with the later development of goitre (swelling of the thyroid gland). The goitre is usually a simple swelling but it may become overactive (hyperthyroidism) or underactive (hypothyroidism). The swelling can become very large and require surgery.

Waardenberg's Syndrome (1951)

Deafness is associated with pigmentary abnormalities which include a white forelock, retinal pigmentation and heterochromia of the irises. The eyes are widely spaced and there are epicanthic folds.

Usher's Syndrome (1914)

There are several syndromes which include both deafness and visual impairment. The commonest is Usher's syndrome. This is characterised by congenital deafness and retinitis pigmentosa. Retinitis pigmentosa is a degenerative condition of the retina which leads, at first, to night blindness and then to progressive restriction of the visual fields (tunnel vision).

The inheritance of Usher's syndrome varies from family to family because different genes are involved. Sometimes a dominant gene is responsible so that children of affected parents also have the syndrome.

The presentation of Usher's syndrome varies. Some children with Usher's syndrome are born partially deaf but most are profoundly deaf. The commonest presentation is that of congenital profound deafness with the insidious onset of the visual problems in late childhood or early adolescence.

Deafness and optic atrophy

There are several syndromes which include deafness and optic atrophy. Some of these are transmitted in an autosomal dominant manner.

Klippel-Fiel Syndrome (McLay and Maran 1969)

This syndrome is characterised by a short neck due to fusion of the cervical vertebrae. The neck is webbed and immobile. Deafness is a common feature.

Alport's Syndrome (1927)

Deafness begins in later childhood and is associated with nephritis. It is more common in boys than in girls.

Treacher-Collins Syndrome (1900)

There is deformity of the external ears. The pinnae are usually small and malformed and the external meatus is narrow. The ossicles of the middle ear are also malformed.

Jerval, Lange-Nielson Syndrome (1957)

This is an uncommon but important syndrome because it can be a cause of sudden death in childhood or in adolescence. The syndrome consists of congenital deafness associated with sudden episodes of loss of consciousness due to a defect in the conductive mechanism of the heart. The cardiac defect is detected by electro-cardiography which shows a characteristic prolongation of the Q-T interval. Cardiac massage during an attack may save life and prophylactic treatment with beta blocking agents may prevent attacks. A cardiac pacemaker should be considered whenever a child is found to have this condition.

BN was referred at the age of 19 years with a history of immature and occasionally aggressive behaviour.

B had been born profoundly deaf but no cause had been found. He had attended a school for deaf children which adopted a purely oral approach to communication. However, he never learned to speak and his scholastic achievements were poor. His parents had been advised by his teachers to talk to him and not under any circumstance to use their hands. They were told that if they were tempted to do so they should sit on their hands.

B had always been prone to temper tantrums and attention seeking behaviour. His work record was poor. He was frequently absent and he was a poor time-keeper. He had had a small number of 'blackouts'. Electroencephalography had shown no abnormality but he was thought to suffer from idiopathic epilepsy.

B was a tall, athletic young man who smiled readily. He attempted to speak but his speech was unintelligible. His verbal language was poor. He was able to communicate at a very basic level by sign language and, within the limits of his verbal language, by fingerspelling. When first addressed using sign language he responded, using sign language, 'I don't like sign language. I don't like deaf people'!

B appeared to be of average or low/average intelligence and it seemed that his behavior problems could be explained on the basis of delayed maturation due to inappropriate educational methods. His parents had not witnessed any of his blackouts but there was no history of prodromata and no abnormal movements had ever been seen. An electrocardiogram revealed a prolonged Q-T interval.

B's parents were advised to take lessons in sign language and to attempt to persuade their son to attend the local deaf club. Unfortunately, some time later, he collapsed and died suddenly while travelling on a bus.

Refsum's Syndrome (1946)

Refsum's Syndrome is a relatively uncommon condition. It is a hereditary disorder of lipid metabolism characterised by peripheral neuropathy, deafness, ataxia and retinal changes.

The author attended a case conference at a mental hospital on a 24-year-old man. He had presented with depression which was attributed to progressive deafness and difficulty in walking. His general practitioner and the consultant were puzzled because although his symptoms appeared to be organic in nature no cause could be found. Moreover, it was thought that his ataxia might be 'hysterical'.

The patient was markedly ataxic and had a considerable degree of deafness. He was depressed, he said, because nobody seemed to understand his symptoms. Further examination revealed some peripheral neuropathy and retinitis pigmentosa.

Those present were impressed when the author suggested that the diagnosis was almost certainly Refsum's syndrome. Subsequent investigations revealed that a younger sister was also losing her hearing, that the patient's blood contained a high level of phytanic acid and that the cerebrospinal fluid showed a marked increase in protein, confirming that diagnosis. It was quite fortuitous that the author had learned of the existence of the disease only the previous evening when reading a medical journal!

Deafness, ichthyosis and keratitis

Congenital deafness may be associated with ichthyosis and keratitis. The following case history illustrates the need for proper assessment and management.

PD. The secretary of a Spastics Group suggested to a consultant paediatrician that a 17-year-old youth should be referred, following a lecture by the author. The young man was about to leave school and, although arrangements had been made for him to attend a 'work centre', there was concern that he had 'very little communication'.

P was born profoundly deaf and with a number of abnormalities which included a slight left hemiparesis, ichthyosis and keratitis. His ichthyosis was of such a degree that if he flexed his joints the skin of his flexures would crack and bleed and he was forced to use a wheel chair. His keratitis gradually became worse and his corneas required 'scraping'. Eventually he had no useful vision.

P had been examined by a number of specialists including a professor of Audiology and Education of the Deaf and had been placed in a residential school for deaf children. The school adopted an aural/oral only policy in the classrooms. Outside classes it allowed the children to use finger spelling and sign language. There were no programmes for staff or parents in sign language.

P's final school report, written in 1973, was as follows

Daily care

Each morning creams are applied to scalp, face, arms, legs and feet. Stockinette and elastic bandages are applied to both legs.

Each evening a bath followed by the application of all creams and ointments as before.

Three times per week hair is washed with a specific shampoo, dry skin is scraped off scalp and ointment is applied. Each lunchtime P rests with his legs up for 30 minutes to an hour.

Each night P sleeps in a bed with the feet substantially raised.

He does not take part in any physical activities. P cannot walk very far — his legs are too heavy. He can use his hands fairly well but they are swollen and he cannot manage fine work.He must avoid standing for long periods, walking for long periods, strong sunlight to head and eyes. He ought not to handle chemicals or gritty substances nor should he have his hands in water except for washing. He must avoid excessive heat and cold. When cracks appear in the skin of his hands and feet, creams must be applied to minimise the chances of infection and bandages applied.

Hearing

Audiometric tests indicate that P has a profound loss of hearing. Even with amplified hearing he cannot understand speech.

Lipreading

P watches faces but has little confidence in his ability to understand. He can lipread a few words and phases but lipreading will not be the most effective way of communicating with him.

Speech

Very rarely uses his voice and such speech as he possesses is virtually unintelligible.

Communication

P's main means of communication is gesture. Occasionally he will use a conventional sign. Fingerspelling is difficult for him because of (a) the condition of his hands and (b) the paucity of his vocabulary and language development.

Intelligence

P gives the impression of being well below average in intellectual development.

Attainments

P's attainments in number, language and all School subjects are abysmally low. He can count up to twenty and has a small vocabulary which helps him to keep in touch with the meaning of very simple written blackboard stories.

Home Circumstances

> *P is lucky to have loving, caring parents and a good home. His parents, however, find it more difficult than the trained nurse at school to ensure that the full regime of treatment is strictly applied. This is no way a criticism: I have every admiration for them.*

Social and Emotional Development

> *P is operating as a much younger child both socially and emotionally. His interests and play patterns are immature.*

Conclusions

> *P is a very severely handicapped boy who will require skilled and regular physical care. He has severe communication problems, his intelligence is below average and his attainments very poor. On the credit side, he has an appealing personality and the ability to make himself popular.*

Recommendations

> *I think it is very unlikely that P will be able to compete in an open labour market unless an employer could be found who would provide him with a repetitive sedentary job in conditions in which his physical, handicaps would be catered for.*

> *Headmaster*

P proved to be a most pleasant young man. He had no useful hearing and very little vision. He had some facility in sign language and was able to make his needs known. He had very limited verbal language and was able to perform only very simple arithmetical tasks. His parents had received no counselling or guidance regarding communication. It was impossible to assess his intelligence but he did not appear to be impaired. Before he lost his vision he could look after himself and find his way about. After full discussion his parents decided to acquire sign language skills and said they would then try to improve their son's literacy.

INSTITUTIONS AND ORGANISATIONS FOR DEAF PEOPLE

NATIONAL AND REGIONAL ORGANISATIONS

The British Deaf Association
38 Victoria Place
Carlisle
Cumbria CA1 1HU
Tel: 0228 48844 (voice/Minicom) 0228 28719 (Qwerty 300 Baud)

The Royal National Institute for the Deaf
105 Gower Street
London WC1E 6AH
Tel: 071 387 8033

RNID North
30 Broad Street
Salford
Manchester M6 5BY
Tel: 061 745 7875 (voice/Minicom) 061 452 7879 (Qwerty)

RNID Midlands
4 Church Road
Edgbaston
Birmingham B15 3TD
Tel: 021 455 6835 (voice/Minicom) 021 452 1071 (QWERTY)

RNID North East
(Sub-Regional Office)
Dene House
Seaham Road
Ryhope
Nr Sunderland SR2 0NP
Tel: 091 523 7647 (voice) 091 523 7648 (Minicom)

RNID South West
138 Church Farm Business Park
Corston
Bath
Avon BA2 9AP
Tel: 0225 874460 (voice/Minicom) 0225 874246 (Fax)

RNID South East
Dike House
1 Malet Street
London WC1E 7JA
Tel: 071 436 3908 (voice/Minicom) 071 436 4430 (Fax)

RNID Northern Ireland
Wilton House
3 College Street North
Belfast BT1 6AR
Tel: 0232 239619 (voice/Minicom) 0232 312032 (Fax)

RNID Scotland
9 Clairmont Gardens
Glasgow G3 7LW
Tel: 041 332 0343 (voice) 041 332 5023 (text)

National Deaf Children's Society
45 Hereford Road
London W2 5AH
Tel: 01 229 9272/4

Sense
The National Association for Deaf-Blind and Rubella Handicapped
311 Gray's Inn Road
London WC1X 8PI
Tel: 071-278-1005 (voice/Qwerty)

Sense-in-Scotland
Glasgow Centre for the Deaf
51 Tobago Street
Glasgow G40 2RH
Tel: 041-556-4808

British Association of the Hard of Hearing
7-11 Armstrong Road
London W3 7JL
Tel: 01 743 1110

RNID Tinnitus Helpline
Unit 2, Pelham Court
Nottingham
NG5 4AP
Tel: 0345 090210 (voice/Minicom)

Type/talk
Pauline Ashley House
Ravenside Retail Park
Speke Road
Liverpool L24 8QB
Tel: 051 494 1000 (voice) 051 494 1022 (Fax)

National Union of the Deaf
288 Bedfont Lane
Feltham
Middlesex TW14 9NU

National Association of Deafened People
103 Heath Road
Widnes
Cheshire WA8 7NU

Council for the Advancement of Communication
   with Deaf People
Pelaw House
School of Education
University of Durham
Durham DH1 1TA
Tel: 091 374 3607

Royal Association in Aid of the Deaf and Dumb
27 Old Oak Road
London W3 7AN
Tel: 01 743 6187

Link
The British Centre for Deafened People
19 Hartfield Road
Eastbourne
East Sussex BN21 2AR

Keep Deaf Children Safe
Margaret Kennedy, Coordinator
c/o Nuffield Hearing and Speech Centre
Grays Inn Road
London WC1X ODA
Tel: 071-833-5627

The Association For All Speech Impaired Children (AFASIC)
347 Central Markets
Smithfield
London
Tel: 01-236-3632/6487

The National Autistic Society
276 Willesden Lane London
NW2 5RB
081 451 1114

Scottish Association of Sign Language Interpreters
1/2 Water Close
Edinburgh EH3 6RB
Tel: 0312 557 0419

PSYCHIATRIC SERVICES

The John Denmark Unit
Mental Health Services of Salford NHS Trust
Bury New Road
Prestwich M25 7BL
Tel: 061 773 2121

Supra Regional Mental Health Service for Deaf People
Springfield Hospital
61 Glenburnie Road
London SW17 7DJ
Tel: 081 784 2707

The Deaf Unit
Denmark House
Queen Elizabeth Psychiatric Hospital
Mindelsohn Way
Edgbaston
Birmingham
B15 2QZ

European Society for Mental Health and Deafness
PO BOX 754
3500 AT Utrecht
Holland

INTERPRETER UNITS

RNID North Regional Interpreter Unit
30 Broad Street
Salford
Manchester M6 5BY
Tel: 061 745 9128 (voice) 061 745 8443 (Fax) 061 745 7822 (T)

RNID East Sussex Interpreter Unit
Warwick House
Warwick Road
Seaford
East Sussex BN 1RG
Tel: 0323 892484 (voice) 0323 874246 (Fax)

RNID Wessex Interpreter Unit
see RNID South West

RNID Northern Ireland Interpreter Unit
see RNID Northern Ireland

Devon and Cornwall Interpreter Unit
Pounds House
Outlands Road
Peverell
Plymouth PL2 3PX
Tel: 0752 780454 (voice/Minicom) 0752 780457 (Fax)

RNID Nottingham Interpreter Unit
2 Pelham Court
Pelham Road
Nottingham NG5 1AP
Tel: 0602 693120 (voice) 0602 693600 (Minicom) 0602 608374 (Fax)

SUGGESTED FORMAT FOR
A SOCIAL HISTORY

1. PERSONAL DETAILS OF CLIENT

Name..

Date of birth..

Address...

Marital status...

Religion...

General practitioner   Name...........................

                         Address........................

                         Telephone......................

Social worker   Name...........................

                         Address........................

                         Telephone......................

Next of kin   Relationship ....

                         Name...........................

                         Address........................

                         Telephone......................

Contact person   Name...........................

                         Address........................

                         Telephone......................

2. INFORMANT

Name..

Status...

Address...

Telephone number......................................

Role..

Duration of involvement...............................

3. DEAFNESS (or Communication disorder)

Degree (functional hearing ability, with or without aids) . . . .
. . . .
Age of onset . . . .
Cause, if known . . . .
Family history . . . .
Disabilities, if any . . . .

4. COMMUNICATION

Preferred modes. . . . .
Facility in those modes . . . .
Degree of literacy . . . .

5. PRESENTING PROBLEM(S)

(A brief account of reason(s) for referral) . . . .
. . . .

6. PREVIOUS ILLNESSES (including hospitalisation)

Physical . . . .
Mental . . . .

7. FAMILY HISTORY

Father   Name. . . . .
                Age . . . .
                Occupation . . . .
Mother   Name. . . . .
                Age . . . .
                Occupation . . . .
Siblings . . . .

Other significant family members

                    Relationship . . . .

                    Name. . . . .

                    Age . . . .

                    Occupation . . . .

Family history of mental disorder. . . . .

8. PERSONAL HISTORY

Birth. . . . .

Infancy (developmental milestones). . . . .

Education. . . . .

Employment . . . .

Intelligence . . . .

Personality. . . . .

Attitudes . . . .

Interests and hobbies. . . . .

Relationships . . . .

Sexual development. . . . .

Alcoholism or drug abuse . . . .

9. HISTORY OF PRESENT CONDITION or REASON FOR REFERRAL

. . . .

. . . .

10. MEDICATION

History. . . . .

Current medication . . . .

11. FURTHER COMMENTS

NB

(a) Lack of information should not prevent referral

(b) A brief letter may suffice in some instances. For example, a client may request a referral and not wish a social history to be compiled.

GLOSSARY

A

Acoustic neuroma
A tumour of the sheath of the 8th cranial nerve

Aetiology
Cause

Affective disorder
see Manic-depressive disease

Akathisia
A form of restlessness in which the subject is unable to remain still for any length of time

Ameslan
The sign language used by the deaf population of the USA

Anarthria
Inability to speak due to disturbance of control of the muscles involved in articulation

Ankylosing spondylitis
A disease of the spinal vertebrae, which become fused together

Anoxia
Lack of oxygen

Aphasia
Inability to speak resulting from damage to the motor speech area of the brain

Aphonia
Inability to speak due to a lesion affecting the function of the vocal chords

Apraxia
Lack of ability to perform familiar actions

Approved Social Worker
A social worker who has been approved under the Mental Health Act 1983 as having appropriate competence in dealing with persons who are suffering from mental disorder.

Athetosis
Slow, writhing, involuntary movements, mainly affecting the upper limbs. Commonly seen in infantile cerebral palsy

Atrophy
Wasting of tissue or organ

Audiogram	Graphic representation of the results of audiometry
Audiometry	The assessment of hearing by an audiometer
Aural/Auditory	Pertaining to the ear or hearing
Autism	*see* Infantile autism

B

Bipolar affective disorder	Manic-depressive disease can present as depression or mania. When there are phases of both mania and depression the term 'bipolar' is often used.
Braille	A system of printing using raised letters which enables blind people to read by touch
British sign language	The sign language used by the deaf population of the British Isles

C

Central language disorder	*see* specific language disorder
Chorea	Involuntary jerky movements of the hands, face and limbs
Choreo-athetosis	A condition on which both athetoid and choreoform movements occur
Cochlea	The shell-shaped organ of hearing in the inner ear
Conductive deafness	Deafness due to pathology of the outer or middle ear
Congenital	Present from birth
Cretinism	A condition occuring in early childhood consisting of delayed growth and mental retardation which is due to deficiency of thyroid hormone in foetal or early life. The skin is thick, wrinkled, sallow and dry. The tongue is large and protruding. The face is broad. The nose is short with a flattened bridge and the forehead is furrowed. The feet and hands are puffy and the abdomen is often protuberant

D

Deaf/blind alphabet	The manual alphabet used by deaf/blind people
Delusion	A false belief
Dysarthria	Difficulty in articulation
Dyskinesia	Impairment of voluntary control causing movements that are incomplete or only partial
Dyslexia	A condition in which an individual with normal intelligence and normal vision is unable to understand written language
Dysphasia	difficulty in speaking due to damage to the motor speech area of the brain
Dysphonia	Difficulty in voice production due to malfunction of the vocal chords
Dyspraxia	Difficulty in performing purposeful movements, the nature of which the individual understands, in the absence of motor paralysis, sensory loss and ataxia
Dysrhythmia	Abnormal rhythm

E

Echolalia	The meaningless reiteration of words or phrases of another person's speech
Echopraxia	The meaningless imitation of gestures, signing, or fingerspelling of another person
Electroencephalography	The study of the electrical activity of the brain
Epigastrium	The upper, central area of the abdomen

F

Fingerspelling	The depicting of letters of the alphabet by using different configurations and movements of the fingers

G

Gastrectomy	Removal of the stomach by surgery
Gesture	Movement of hands, arms or body to express meaning
Goitre	Swelling of the thyroid gland
Glue ear	see Serous otitis media

H

Hallucination	A perception in the absence of an obvious stimulus
Haptic	Pertaining to the sense of touch. Tactile
Hemiplegia	Paralysis of one side of the body
Hereditary	Familial. The transmission of characteristics to descendants
Heterochromia	Of different colours
Hypomania	An abnormal mental state characterised by elevation of mood and psychic and motor overactivity, but not amounting to mania
Hypothyroidism	Underfunctioning of the thyroid gland

I

Ichthyosis	Dryness of the skin
Idiopathic	Of no apparent cause
Idiosyncratic sign language	A system of signs developed independently by a small group of people to overcome communication difficulties
Infantile autism	Childhood psychosis leading to a failure to develop/maintain speech

J

Jervell, Lange-Nielson syndrome	*see page 139*

K

Keratitis	Inflammation of the cornea
Kernicterus	Brain damage due to excessive accumulation of bilirubin in certain parts of the brain which may cause athetosis, spasticity and mental impairment
Klippel-Fiel syndrome	*see page 139*

L

Language	A system of sounds, symbols or signs used for communication
Laryngology	Study and treatment of diseases of the larynx
Lipoma	A tumour consisting of fatty tissue
Lipreading	The understanding of speech by observing the movements of the mouth and lips
Literacy	The ability to communicate effectively by reading and writing

M

Meatus	Passage or opening
Makaton	A vocabulary of signs taken from British Sign Language for use with mentally impaired deaf people
Mania	An abnormal state of elevation of mood which occurs in manic-depressive illness. It is usually associated with psycho- motor overactivity and delusions of grandeur
Manic depressive illness	An illness characterised by periods of depression and elevation of mood
Melaena	Blood in the stools
Mime	Communication by facial expression and bodily posture and movement
Myopia	Short sightedness
Moon	A method of reading by touch used by blind people

Motor aphasia	Inability to speak due to a lesion of the second frontal convolution of the brain
Myxoedema	A disease due to underfunctioning of the thyroid gland in adult life. Characterised by slow and deep speech, dry thickened skin, puffiness of the hands and face, dry thinning hair and eyebrows, and mental apathy.

N

Neologism	A newly invented word.

O

Obsession	An abnormally persistent thought or urge
Optic	Pertaining to the eyes or sight
Oral	By mouth
Ossicles	The small bones, the malleus, the incus and the stapes, which transmit sounds from the tympanum to the oval window
Otitis	Inflammation of the ear
Otosclerosis	A form of deafness due to fixation of the stapes of the middle ear by bony deposits

P

Passivity	The subjective experience of being influenced by external forces or agencies which is a characteristic of schizophrenia
Pendred's syndrome	*see page 138*
Peptic ulcer	Ulceration of the stomach or duodenum
Perceptive deafness	Deafness due to pathology of the 8th nerve or cochlea
Perinatal	About the time of birth
Phenomenology	The study of the presentation of mental disorder
Pinna	The external part of the ear

Post-lingual	After the development of speech
Precordium	The front of the chest
Prelingual	A term which was used to describe preverbal deafness
Preverbal	A term suggested by the author to describe deafness which is present before the development of verbal language
Presbyacusis	The sensorineural deafness which occurs as part of the normal process of aging
Prodromata	Symptoms which precede the full clinical emergence of an illness
Psycholinguistics	The study of the structure of language and its relation to the workings of the mind
Psychometry	Psychological assessment
Psychosis	A form of mental disorder in which most patients lose contact with reality

Q

Quadriplegia	Paralysis of all four limbs

R

Refsum's syndrome	*see page 140*
Retinitis Pigmentosa	A degenerative condition of the retina which leads to night blindness, followed by progressive restriction of the visual fields (tunnel vision). *See* Usher's Syndrome, *page 138*
Rhesus incompatibility	*see* kernicterous
Rubella	German measles

S

Schizophrenia	A mental illness characterised by changes in mood, disturbances of thought and volition and abnormal perceptual experiences

Semantics	The branch of linguistics which is concerned with meanings
Sensori-neural deafness	Deafness due to pathology of the cochlea or the eighth cranial nerve
Serous otitis media	the accumulation of serous fluid in the middle ear
Specific language disorder	Inability to understand the meaning of speech due to an abnormality in the receptive language area of the brain
Speech	A method of communication by the vocalisation of verbal language
Surdophrenia	Term coined by Basilier (1964) to describe the behavioural and adjustment problems commonly seen in young deaf people
Syntax	The structure of language

T

Tinnitus	The perception of sound in the absence of an acoustic stimulus

U

Usher's syndrome	*see page 138*

V

Verbal	Pertaining to words. Verbal languages include those which are written or fingerspelt

W

Waardenburg's syndrome	*see page 138*